SWEET & SIMPLE

Also by Christina Lane

Dessert for Two

Comfort and Joy

SWEET & SIMPLE

Dessert For Two

CHRISTINA LANE

THE COUNTRYMAN PRESS
A division of W. W. Norton & Company
Independent Publishers Since 1923

Manufacturing by Quad Graphics, Taunton
Book design by Natalie Olsen, Kisscut Design
Production manager: Devon Zahn

The Countryman Press
www.countrymanpress.com

A division of W. W. Norton & Company
500 Fifth Avenue, New York, NY 10110
www.wwnorton.com

978-1-68268-007-0

10 9 8 7 6 5 4 3 2 1

———— »·« ————

This book is for you. Yes, you. You who hunts down mini bakeware, you who doesn't want tempting leftovers, and you who delights in the simplicity of a small cake rather than a giant three-layer one. You get me. I do it all for you.

I mean, I get to eat the desserts too, so let's call it a win-win.

I love you more than butter, sugar, and flour.

———— »·« ————

CONTENTS

Introduction

I wrote this book in four-hour increments. When I wrote the first *Dessert for Two*, I was child-free. And now, well, I have a baby and two dogs. Finding the time to write this book was challenging, but I knew it was a worthwhile pursuit. I wanted to do it for *you*.

I still love baking desserts for two, because we still eat dessert for two. Yes, I'm one of those parents withholding sugar from my kid for as long as possible. I know how ridiculous it is, trust me: I was never allowed junk food or dessert as a kid and, well, my career choice speaks for itself, doesn't it?

So, for the most part, this small family still only needs small desserts. This time around, though, I included a chapter at the end with desserts that fit in an 8-inch pan, for slightly more than two servings. The truth is, now that I have the world's most adorable child (heh), we have a lot more visitors these days, and I'm so happy to make larger desserts to feed just a few more than two people.

For the most part, though, this is another small-batch dessert cookbook for you. I divided the chapters by pan size, so you can make one quick run to the hobby store, gather all of your mini pans, and come home and bake everything to your heart's content.

You'll notice some slightly healthier desserts here. You're shocked, I know. I included some light, fruit-centered desserts because I just don't think there's anything better than a dessert made with ripe, local, seasonal fruit. I also ventured into the world of "naturally sweetened" desserts. I did this mainly for my daughter. She's getting to the age where she wants whatever Mom and Dad are eating. I try to meet her demands/tantrums with desserts made with maple syrup, honey, and coconut sugar. Sugar is sugar, yes, but it lessens the mom guilt. (Anything that lessens mom guilt is a very good thing.)

I'm so happy you're here again, and I couldn't be more proud to share more small-batch desserts with you.

As always, I'm pretty easy to find on the Internet, and I absolutely love it when you reach out to me with requests. I'll always be here, scaling down giant desserts to more manageable portions. It's just what I was put on this earth to do.

*Love and
(a small batch of) cupcakes,*
Christina

Ingredients Guide

Butter is my sidekick. I frequently indulge in rich, European butter because I'm a woman who would rather shop at the grocery store than the mall. That said, I tested all of these recipes with regular, store-brand butter to be sure they would work. American butter typically has a higher water content than imported butter, but you're safe using either for my recipes. The best way to soften butter is to leave it on the counter for two hours. If you're in a rush (or just impatient like me), slice the butter into small pieces and leave it on the counter for 20 minutes. Softened butter is just one notch above room

temperature. You can press your finger into it and make an indentation, but it is not overly soft or droopy. You finger should not go all the way through, and you should most definitely not use melted butter when a recipe calls for softened butter. To be more clear: do not use the microwave to soften butter. Do what I do: chop it small and let it rest while you gather and prepare the ingredients for the recipe.

Flour is always bleached, all-purpose.

Refrigerated premade pie dough helps me put the "simple" in *Sweet & Simple*. I think every pie I ever ate growing up was made with pie dough from the red box. I have a soft spot for it in my heart, but if you want to make your own crust, check my recipe for Strawberry Hand Pies (page 32).

Cornstarch might be a new ingredient in your kitchen. I use it to make cakes super fluffy (especially the Angel Food Jam Cake, page 48), and to thicken fruit fillings in pies.

Sugar is always white, granulated sugar, unless it specifically says brown sugar. There was a time when I always used light brown sugar in desserts, but recently I've ventured over to the dark side—dark **brown sugar** is rocking my world. The only difference between light and dark brown sugar is additional molasses. If you love spice and smoky molasses as much as me, more of it is always a good thing.

Molasses is a fun ingredient in fall recipes, but anytime I use it, I reach for regular molasses, not blackstrap. I think blackstrap molasses has a pronounced bitter flavor that does not go well in baked goods. You're looking for regular molasses when baking.

Wanna talk about **coconut sugar**? I've found it to be widely available these days, and I love it so much. The best way to describe it is like regular white sugar, but with a little extra depth and spice. Once you make the Coconut Sugar Cookies (page 16), you'll understand—the cookies taste like they have so many ingredients, but it's really just the coconut sugar bringing so much flavor to the table.

Coarse grain sugar is perfect for sprinkling on scone cookies, mini pies, and more. It's just so pretty! It's entirely optional, but once you use it, you'll be

hooked. I buy Sugar in the Raw, and I love its earthy brown color too.

Maple syrup has become my go-to sweetener in the morning for coffee and tea. I buy the big jugs at Costco and it finds its way into cream cheese frosting, cupcakes, and more.

Salt is always fine, natural sea salt.

Baking powder and **baking soda** speak for themselves, but I want to remind you to check their expiration dates. These ingredients are critical to giving our desserts rise and lift, and if they're outdated, well, they just won't work properly.

Eggs are always large, Grade A eggs. Speaking of eggs, I want to remind you that since we're baking small batches, I often only call for a portion of an egg in a recipe—either the egg yolk or egg white. At the end of the book, I've included a list of ways to use up the remaining portion. I never want eggs to go to waste.

Vanilla, almond, and **peppermint extracts** should be the most fragrant ones you can find. The better they smell, the better your desserts will taste. Though I will admit to occasionally loving the artificial vanilla flavor in cake frosting (it's just so marshmallow-y!), real-deal Bourbon-steeped vanilla is king. I also call for vanilla beans a few times in this book, but know that it's entirely optional. One teaspoon of vanilla extract equals one-third of a vanilla bean, so substitute if necessary.

The same thing goes for **ground spices**. If you want your desserts to taste the best, fresh and fragrant spices are really the way to go. I know that it can be hard to buy huge spice containers when my recipes only call for ⅛ or ¼ teaspoon, so try to buy them in bulk if you can. That way, they stay fresh and you don't have any leftovers (clearly my mission in life is no leftovers).

Can I be slightly demanding and insist that all of your **citrus juices** be freshly squeezed? It just makes such a difference. Bottled lemon juice would be illegal if it were up to me.

When I call for **citrus zest**, I use a Microplane grater. It takes off just the zest and leaves the white, bitter part behind. I use my Microplane almost daily in my kitchen for grating everything from lemons and oranges to chocolate, ginger, and garlic. It's one of those kitchen tools you think you can live without until you have one, and then you'll become obsessed!

Neutral oil is one ingredient that I will not be bossy about. When I call for neutral oil in a recipe, I mean any oil that won't impart any flavor on the baked good. This can be sunflower, canola, vegetable, safflower, or anything you like. The exception is my Olive Oil Cakelets (page 105), which call for a fruity, fragrant olive oil.

Cocoa powder comes in two different, delicious varieties. The most common is natural unsweetened cocoa powder. The other type is dark unsweetened cocoa powder. The two are not interchangeable due to alkalinity issues. I've heard from some folks on the inside that Hershey's dark cocoa powder is interchangeable because it's actually a blend of the two with an alkalinity adjustment, but don't quote me on that. Because there are a few recipes here that explicitly call for **dark cocoa powder** for maximum flavor (Dark Chocolate Cake + Red Wine Syrup, page 161, I'm lookin' at you), I offer a few other ways to use up the rest of the box. You can

always use dark cocoa powder in chocolate frostings for extra depth and flavor.

The best **chocolate** to use is your favorite kind. I most commonly reach for semisweet chips, but a chopped chocolate bar is always welcome.

Sour cream, **heavy cream**, and all dairy products should contain as much fat as possible. Sorry. I don't test my recipes with low-fat or nonfat dairy products because it's just not right. Low-fat dairy products contain unnecessary chemicals that vary between brands. I'd hate for you to have a recipe failure because of it, so always use full-fat sour cream when called for. Along those lines, heavy cream is always heavy whipping cream.

While we're talking about dairy, let's discuss **buttermilk**. I buy it frequently because it's the secret to amazing mashed potatoes, but if you don't keep it around, add ¼ to ½ teaspoon of vinegar to milk, stir, and let sit for 5 minutes. The milk will thicken and become sufficiently acidic to react with the baking soda in the recipe.

Coconut cream is a more flavorful substitution for heavy cream. I won't debate the health benefits here, because calories from fat are roughly the same. I just prefer it because I'm coconuts for coconut products. Canned coconut products can be confusing. On the shelf right now, you'll find light coconut milk, full-fat coconut milk, and coconut cream. I don't call for light or full-fat coconut milk anywhere in this book, though I do make rice and curry with it frequently for dinner. For baking, I'm using nothing but canned coconut cream. Often when you open the can it's a solid mass—especially if you refrigerate it first. I've seen mini 4-ounce cans of this stuff most frequently, but as the culinary uses for coconut cream have expanded, I've seen large 14-ounce cans (hallelujah!). Avoid at all costs "cream of coconut," which is really just sweetened coconut cream. This is for making super sweet cocktails, which are nice, but there are no recipes for those in this book, unfortunately. Maybe next time.

Speaking of coconut, I've started buying **unsweetened shredded coconut** lately, solely because of the baby. If all you can find is sweetened flakes, just reduce the sugar in the recipe a tad—it'll be fine.

So, maybe I have an obsession with coconut products. I call for **coconut oil** a few times in this book, and for good reason—it sets firmly when chilled, while other oils do not. I like this in my Chocolate Fruit Bark (page 98), my Marshmellow-Filled Cupcakes (page 93), and more.

Using unflavored powdered **gelatin** makes me feel like a professional pastry chef. It's really nothing fancy, though. You can find it next to the sweet, flavored versions in the little white box. I use it to make the easiest Easiest Lemon Bars (page 189), and to thicken Coconut Panna Cotta (page 143) and Strawberry Mousse (page 156). If I'm going to make a dessert ahead of time that contains whipped cream, I'll often stir in a teaspoon of gelatin to help it hold up in the fridge. This is true for my Lemon Matcha Cake Roll (page 181).

A few final notes on grains: I stock **rolled oats** in my pantry, and if I need quick oats, I just pulse them in a food processor for 10 seconds. **Almond meal** is simply ground almonds with their skins on. You can make it yourself in the food processor for my Best Ever Jam Bars (page 195). Do not confuse it with pricy almond flour.

Equipment You Will Need

I'd like to go over the specifics of the pan I use for each chapter—and a few other things too. I'll try not to get too bossy.

Measuring

You probably know this, but you're going to need some measuring cups and a few measuring spoons with which to bake. Gosh, I hope you know this! Your measuring cups should start at ¼ cup and go to 1 cup, at minimum. A set with a ⅛ cup is nice, but know that ⅛ cup equals 2 tablespoons.

As for measuring spoons, I want you to seek out ones that go down to a teensy ⅛ teaspoon measure. Picky, picky, I know, but I often call for ⅛ teaspoon of leavener or salt. We are small-batch baking after all, aren't we?

In my spare time (ha, that phrase always makes me laugh!), I teach cooking classes. One of the first things I love to talk about is when to use a liquid measure and when to use a dry measure. The way to measure dry ingredients, like flour and sugar, is with a measuring cup. The way to measure liquid ingredients, like oil and milk, is with a glass measuring cup. See the opposite page for an example of what a glass or liquid measuring cup looks like.

Bakeware

Mini Baking Sheet
It took me a while to realize the value of the mini baking sheet in my kitchen. Sure, I always used it for baking my small-batch cookies, but it wasn't until I used them for mini sheet cakes that I began to see their worth. I like to think that anything that fits on a sheet pan is a pan of love. You can make almost anything for two on it.

I lean towards thin metal baking sheets with a 1-inch lip around the edges. And when given the chance, I'll opt for a lighter colored pan rather than the darker metals. I have a few of each in my kitchen and the light, thin pans bake cookies and cakes the most evenly. It probably goes against your instinct to choose a flimsy pan over a sturdy one, but the heat from the oven moves more easily through lightweight pans.

I have acquired some of these pans through buying sets of baking pans, like a little quarter-sheet pan stacked inside a half-sheet pan. I use my big half-sheet pan for roasting vegetables and my smaller quarter-sheet pans for baking. They even make silicon mats for quarter-sheet baking pans now, which tells me that these little pans are catching on.

Classic Loaf Pan
You could say my love affair with small-batch baking began here. When I realized that anything baked in the loaf pan and cut down the middle happily served two, I started collecting them.

My favorite bread loaf pans measure 9 x 3 inches with a height of about 5 inches. I prefer ones with sharp corners, but mainly only so my bars have prettier edges. I often reach for the metal pans over the heavy ceramic ones, because I've found that they conduct heat more evenly and things bake quicker in them. That doesn't mean you can't use the rounded-edge ceramic bread loaf pan—you absolutely can, but tack on a few extra minutes of baking time. It takes heat longer to permeate a ceramic pan than a metal pan. My mom frequently uses her decorative ceramic pans for my recipes and everything works out just fine.

Wielding a spatula can be tricky in these small pans, so I always line the pan with parchment paper. Leave enough excess paper to form handles, and it'll be a breeze to get your mini bars out of the pan.

The 8-inch and 9-inch bread loaf pan are almost indistinguishable—use your ruler as a guide. The 8-inch pan will be mostly fine, but due to its smaller size, the bars and cakes will need extra baking time.

I have to admit my favorite use for this pan is the mini angel food cake. I used to reserve angel food cake for when I finally had 12 leftover egg whites in the freezer, and had the time and attention span to bake a big tube pan of cake—but now that I'm only using a handful of egg whites and my trusty bread loaf pan, my life has had a lot more angel food cake in it. Considering it's one of my favorite cakes (after tres leches cake!), it's been a very good thing. Life is too short to only eat your favorite cake every once in a while.

Muffin Pan

I really hope you already have one of these pans in your kitchen. I have too many muffins pans in my house. If you're lacking one, come over and you can pick through my teetering tower of metal muffin pans.

I'm especially hard on these pans; mine are covered in scratches, baked on "stuff," and are dented on the edges. I don't know if it's because I use them for things other than baking muffins, but just about every time my Mom comes over for a visit, she tells me I need a new muffin pan. And so I listen to her and go buy one, but then I have a hard time throwing the old one away.

Just when I thought my collection couldn't get any larger, I went to an estate sale in my neighborhood and discovered the most adorable vintage muffin pan with a capacity of only 6 cups. Bashert, is what it is. I pretty much only use that pan now. It's just too cute not to use.

Ramekins

I am a complete "ramekin fanatic." I love them in all shapes, sizes, and colors. In fact, if you ever need to buy my love, buy me a set of matching ramekins—the more unique, the better.

However, in an effort to simplify and standardize, I only used one type of ramekins when testing recipes for this book: the classic 4-ounce crème brûlée ramekin. I can't promise that I have only used white ones, but I can attest to their capacity of 4-ounces only.

The exception to this rule was the Cherry Cobbler (page 108), as pictured on the cover. We all agreed it would best to use a shallow ramekin (still 4 ounces, though!) to best show off those tiny little hearts.

It's helpful to have a crème brûlée torch for a few recipes in this book, so if you see a set for sale with two ramekins and a torch, grab it! That's how I got my start in the ramekin world—a little set of two pink ramekins that came with a mini torch. I still have those tiny ramekins, but I have since upgraded to a full-size culinary torch.

6-inch Round Cake Pan

This might be the only piece of bakeware you will have to seek out for this book. I'm sorry for the extra trip to the store, I truly am, but if you love cake, you'll love making mini cakes. I love the portion control of it all. I love that I can make my favorite 3-layer cake smaller and just enjoy a few slices of it. But most of all, I love that I don't have a lot of leftover cake tempting me in the house. I'm not immune to eating cake for breakfast. It happens to the best of us.

Buying the right 6-inch round cake pan is very important. They come in two sizes now: 2-inches and 3-inches high. The pan you want is 2-inches high. The extra inch on the other pan creates excess heat in the oven, and subsequently might sink your cakes. I've troubleshooted many sunken cakes only to discover the culprit was a too-tall pan.

8-inch Square Pan

Admittedly, this pan hasn't always been in my 'for two' arsenal, because, well, it makes more dessert than two people can eat. However, it makes less than what 6 to 8 people can eat, so I think we should let this cake pan into the family, don't you? I'd say dessert made in an 8-inch square pan serves about 4 people. It's still less than the typical recipes that serve 8+, so I'm happy with it.

I'm glad to welcome these "smaller batch" recipes into the club, because the number one thing you guys love to ask me is if you can double a recipe. Once you find a recipe you love, like say my carrot cake, you want to make a few more servings. I scaled up my famous carrot cake slightly, and shared it with you here (page 172). I hope you love the new twist on the frosting!

Selfishly, I make lemon bars in this pan, because you guys know they're my go-to dessert. I've never met a lemon bar I didn't like, so I'm happy to have a slightly bigger version in an 8-inch square pan.

When it comes to square pans, again, I always reach for metal bakeware. It's just the workhorse in my kitchen. I've always had gas ovens that run hot, so I've found that metal bakeware cooks evenly. My mom almost exclusively bakes in ceramic square pans, so I have it on good word that all of these recipes will work in that pan too.

Utensils

I'm giving you permission to shop for a cute mini whisk, a small flexible spatula, a darling wooden spoon, and more. Go on, get yourself to a kitchen shop!

Hand Mixer

My preference is to stir together dough and batter with a spoon, because I am lazy. But, the times when I do call for a recipe to be beaten, I'm always referring to a small hand-held mixer. A large stand mixer is overkill for small desserts—the paddle spins without touching the batter at the bottom of the bowl. KitchenAid just released a mini version of their stand mixer (called the "Artisan Mini"), and I'm currently vetting it for you now.

I just want to mention that when a batter is beaten with an electric mixer, it is for the distinct purpose of incorporating air and achieving fluffiness. Beating air into butter and sugar is a very good thing. Don't skip or skimp on the process, or your final baked goods will be flat and sad.

Mixing Bowls

I used to buy mixing bowl sets, but I found that I only used the smallest bowl in the group. The rest collected dust in my drawer. So, now I just buy cute vintage bowls when I see them. And heck, some of my recipes I whip up in one of those over-sized coffee mugs. It's just another thing I love about small-batch baking: fewer dishes!

Culinary Torch

There are probably too many recipes here that call for the use of a kitchen torch. But I think you've always wanted one and I'm happy to give you an excuse to buy it. They're fun, and they really lend an undeniably delicious crispy crust to things like crème brûlée, and Baked Alaska.

Parchment Paper

I buy unbleached, made-from-recycled-paper, brown parchment paper because I'm a hipster. On occasion, I use reusable silicone mats instead, but I have found that silicone mats prevent cookies from spreading as much as I would like them to.

I think that covers it. Now, let's get (small batch) baking!

MINI BAKING SHEET

ORANGE CHOCOLATE CHUNK COOKIES

It's not that standard chocolate chip cookies needed to be improved upon; it's that I love the combination of orange and chocolate! With a packed ½ teaspoon of orange zest, these cookies really sing with flavor.

Makes 1 dozen cookies

6 tablespoons
unsalted butter, softened

¼ cup dark brown sugar, packed

3 tablespoons granulated sugar

1 large egg yolk

½ teaspoon vanilla extract

½ teaspoon freshly
grated orange zest

½ cup + 2 tablespoons
all-purpose flour

⅛ teaspoon fine sea salt

¼ teaspoon baking soda

¼ teaspoon baking powder

⅓ cup chocolate chunks

Preheat the oven to 375°F and spray a baking sheet with cooking spray.

In a medium-size bowl, add the butter and beat on medium speed with an electric mixer. Beat for just a few seconds to break it up and make it lightly fluffy, about 10 seconds.

Add the brown sugar and granulated sugar to the butter and beat until fluffy, about 45 seconds.

Next, add the egg yolk, vanilla, and orange zest to the bowl, and beat until combined.

Evenly sprinkle the flour, salt, baking soda, and baking powder on top, and beat until just combined—do not overmix.

Finally, stir in the chocolate chunks by hand. Scrape the bottom of the bowl well to ensure all of the flour is incorporated.

Divide the dough into 12 balls and space them evenly on the prepared baking sheet.

Bake for 8 minutes and check them—the cookies should be golden on the edges. If not, return to the oven for up to 2 more minutes, but be careful not to overbake or they will lose their chewy centers.

Let the cookies cool on the sheet pan for 1 minute before moving to a wire rack to cool completely before serving.

Who am I kidding? Eat these babies warm!

EASY CHOCOLATE HAZELNUT COOKIES

You look like you need a cookie. In fact, I think you should definitely have a cookie in your hand while reading this book. This cookie is your best bet—it comes together quickly in one bowl with ingredients you already have, and you don't even have to use a mixer! You can have a warm chocolate hazelnut cookie in your hands in 11 minutes if you're extra quick.
Makes 6 cookies

½ cup chocolate hazelnut spread

¼ cup granulated sugar

1 large egg

½ cup all-purpose flour

¼ cup chocolate chips

Sea salt, for sprinkling

Preheat the oven to 350°F.

Stir together all ingredients (except sea salt) in a medium-size bowl with a spoon (do not use a mixer).

Scoop out six portions of dough onto a baking sheet.

Bake for 10 minutes. Immediately upon removing from the oven, sprinkle sea salt on top. Let cool for 2 minutes on the pan and then move to a wire rack to cool completely, if you can resist. Mmmm, melted chocolate hazelnut fudge centers!

COCONUT SUGAR COOKIES

Have you seen coconut sugar in your store yet? I discovered it at Trader Joe's one day, and I grabbed a bag. I'm all for using natural sugars in dessert. . . but only so we can eat more dessert—I mean, let's be open and honest with one another.

The thing I love about baking with coconut sugar is that it brings its own unique flavor to the party. Even though these are plain sugar cookies, they have hints of caramel and nuttiness from the coconut sugar. It's like more flavor for less effort. Spice cookies without the spice? Have I sold you yet?

Makes 1 dozen cookies

6 tablespoons unsalted butter, at room temperature

½ cup + 2 tablespoons coconut sugar

1 large egg

½ teaspoon vanilla

1 cup all-purpose flour

1 teaspoon baking soda

¼ teaspoon fine sea salt

Preheat the oven to 375°F and line a baking sheet with parchment paper.

In a medium-size bowl, beat together the butter, coconut sugar, egg, and vanilla.

Sprinkle the flour, baking soda, and salt on top, and beat until combined.

Scoop generous tablespoonfuls of the dough onto the prepared baking sheet and bake for 8 to 10 minutes, or until the tops of the cookies look dry.

Let cool on the pan for 1 minute, then move to a wire rack to cool completely.

Serve immediately, or keep covered in a storage container so that they stay soft.

If you're not familiar with "Lofthouse" cookies, let me assure you: These are the best sugar cookies ever. I'm sure you've had them before—they're usually in the grocery store near the checkout, and they're always brightly colored and piled high with sprinkles. They are hard to resist.

But actually, they became really easy for me to resist once I took a quick glance at the ingredient list. These cookies are much, much better home-made.

The cookies are slightly puffy, tender, and melt-in-your-mouth delicious. The frosting on top isn't optional—it's the pinnacle of perfect buttercream. Pull out your favorite sprinkles and decorate with abandon. And on that note, switch up the sprinkles to make these match any holiday throughout the year! *Makes 6 cookies*

LOFTHOUSE COOKIES

FOR THE COOKIES:

3 tablespoons unsalted butter, at room temperature

⅓ cup granulated sugar

1 large egg yolk

4 tablespoons heavy cream

1 teaspoon vanilla extract

1 cup all-purpose flour

½ teaspoon baking powder

⅛ teaspoon fine sea salt

FOR THE FROSTING:

5 tablespoons unsalted butter, at room temperature

¾ cup powdered sugar

½ teaspoon vanilla extract

½ teaspoon heavy cream

Sprinkles!

EASY TIP: *Say you want to make these cookies, but you don't have cream. I hear ya. It happens to me all the time. I stirred in whole milk once, and the batter was way too soft to make cookies. BUT, I put the dough in the fridge for just 15 minutes, went on to make them anyway, and they were just fine! The cookies are best with heavy cream, but if all you have is milk, it will still work.*

First, preheat the oven to 350°F and line a baking sheet with a silicone liner. (In my experience, silicone liners prevent cookies from overspreading.)

In a medium-size bowl, add the butter and beat on medium speed with an electric mixer. Beat for about 10 seconds to break it up.

Add the sugar to the butter and beat until fluffy, about 45 seconds.

Next, add the egg yolk, heavy cream, and vanilla. Beat until just combined.

Evenly sprinkle the flour, baking powder, and salt over the batter, and beat until just combined.

The dough will be a little softer than regular cookies, but you should still be able to work with it. (See note about using milk below).

Press the dough down into the bottom of the bowl and use your hand to lightly score it in half. From each half of dough, you should get three balls of dough.

Place each dough ball in your hands and roll it to make a perfect ball. Place each ball, evenly spaced, on the prepared baking sheet.

Press the dough balls to flatten them slightly.

Bake for 14 to 15 minutes. The tops will appear dry when they're done.

Let the cookies cool on the baking sheet for 1 minute before moving to a wire rack to cool completely.

Meanwhile, mix together all of the frosting ingredients (except the sprinkles!) in a bowl using an electric mixer on medium-high speed.

Frost the cookies once they've cooled and decorate with sprinkles.

GOOEY BUTTER CAKE COOKIES

4 ounces cream cheese, softened

4 tablespoons unsalted butter, softened

¾ cup granulated sugar

½ teaspoon vanilla extract

1 large egg + 1 large egg yolk

1 cup + 2 tablespoons all-purpose flour

1 teaspoon baking powder

¼ + ⅛ teaspoon fine sea salt

⅓ cup powdered sugar

In a medium-size bowl, add the cream cheese and butter. Beat together with an electric mixer until fluffy, about 30 seconds.

Slowly add the sugar to the cream cheese mixture while continuously beating. Beat the sugar into the cream cheese mixture until light and fluffy, 1 minute.

Next, add the vanilla, whole egg, and egg yolk. Beat until combined.

In a separate small bowl, whisk together the flour, baking powder, and salt. Add this to the cream cheese mixture in three even increments, beating in between each addition.

Cover the dough tightly and chill in the fridge for at least 1 hour, and up to overnight. Do not skip this step.

Preheat the oven to 325°F and line a baking sheet with parchment paper.

Have the powdered sugar ready in a shallow bowl nearby.

Scoop out 2 tablespoons of dough and roll it in your hands to form a ball. Repeat with remaining dough until you have 12 to 13 balls. Roll each ball in powdered sugar before placing them on the baking sheet, evenly spaced, at least 2 inches from each other.

Bake for 14 minutes. Keep a close eye on these cookies—they should not brown in the oven. The tops of the cookies will be puffed and slightly wet. Let the cookies cool completely on the baking sheet before serving.

Have you ever had gooey butter cake? It's a soft cake topped with a gooey, rich buttery topping. Yes, it's exactly as good as it sounds. Everyone who eats it says, "Oh, this is too sweet," but they end up going on to eat a sizable portion. "Too sweet" is just something you say about gooey butter cake, or these gooey butter cake cookies, just like eating too many of them is just something you do. *Makes 1 dozen cookies*

PEANUT BUTTER CHOCOLATE CHIP COOKIES

Need a quick batch of cookies? *Makes 1 dozen cookies*

4 tablespoons
unsalted butter, softened

⅓ cup natural peanut butter

¾ cup + 2 tablespoons
dark brown sugar

1 large egg

1 teaspoon vanilla extract

1 cup all-purpose flour

¾ teaspoon baking powder

¼ teaspoon baking soda

½ teaspoon fine sea salt

1 cup chocolate chunks (or chips)

Preheat the oven to 350°F and line a baking sheet with a silicone mat or parchment paper.

In a medium-size bowl, beat together the butter, peanut butter, and brown sugar with an electric mixer on medium speed. Beat until thoroughly blended and lightly fluffy, about 40 seconds.

Next, add the egg and vanilla and beat until combined.

Sprinkle the flour, baking powder, baking soda, and salt evenly over the dough.

Beat until just combined.

Finally, stir in the chocolate chunks.

Press the dough flat in the bowl and roughly divide it in quarters by eye (you can also lightly score it with a knife).

Make three dough balls out of each quarter of dough (for a total of 12 cookies).

Roll the dough balls lightly in your hands and then place them on the baking sheet, evenly spaced.

Bake for 11 minutes. The edges will start to brown, but the centers will still appear soft.

Let the cookies cool on the baking sheet for 1 minute before moving them to a wire rack to cool completely.

PERFECT SUGAR COOKIES

And I really mean perfect—I love that this small-batch recipe makes just 10 cookies. *Makes 10 cookies*

4 tablespoons
unsalted butter, melted

⅓ cup granulated sugar

1 large egg yolk

½ teaspoon vanilla extract

½ cup + 3 tablespoons
all-purpose flour

¼ teaspoon baking soda

⅛ teaspoon fine sea salt

Preheat the oven to 350°F and prepare baking sheet pan, lining it with parchment or spraying it with cooking spray.

Stir together the melted butter, sugar, egg yolk, and vanilla. Stir until very well mixed.

Next, sprinkle the flour, baking powder, and salt evenly over the top of the dough.

Stir until just combined.

Divide the dough in half by eye and make five dough balls out of each half.

Space the dough balls evenly on a baking sheet and bake for 8 to 10 minutes.

The cookies will be puffy when they come out of the oven, but they will flatten slightly and crack as they cool.

BLACKBERRY SCONE COOKIES

These cookies are like a mash-up of strawberry shortcake: the tender not-too-sweet biscuit, the fresh berries, the crusty edges—it's all here.

My daughter's favorite combination is blackberries and coconut sugar, but feel free to mix it up and use strawberries and regular sugar. If you use strawberries, double the amount.

These cookies aren't too sweet, and that's exactly what I love about them. They're great for breakfast or an afternoon snack with a toddler who just woke up from a nap. *Makes 1 dozen cookies*

3 ounces fresh blackberries (a handful)

1 cup all-purpose flour

1 teaspoon baking powder

¼ teaspoon fine sea salt

⅓ cup coconut sugar

3 tablespoons cold unsalted butter

⅓ cup + 1 tablespoon heavy cream

Coarse sanding sugar for topping (optional)

First, preheat the oven to 350°F and line a baking sheet with parchment paper or a silicone mat.

Next, slice the blackberries in half or quarter them, depending on size.

In a medium-size bowl, combine the flour, baking powder, salt, and sugar. Stir with a fork until well blended.

Next, add the butter and cut it into the mixture using two knives or a pastry blender. Work the butter in until it's evenly dispersed and is smaller than peas.

Add the heavy cream and stir gently until a dough forms.

Sprinkle in the blackberries and fold gently to combine.

Scoop 12 balls of dough onto the baking sheet (or make six larger cookies) and top with a sprinkling of coarse sugar (if using). Bake the cookies for 20 to 25 minutes.

Immediately move the cookies to a wire rack to cool completely before serving. The cookies soften as they rest so they're best when served the same day.

SUGAR COOKIE
FRUIT PIZZA

If there's anything better than sharing a giant sugar cookie, it's slathering it with orange cream cheese frosting and topping it with fresh fruit. This mini fruit pizza cuts into four little slices. *Makes one 4-slice pizza*

3 tablespoons
unsalted butter, softened

¼ cup granulated sugar

1 large egg yolk

½ teaspoon vanilla extract

½ cup all-purpose flour

⅛ teaspoon baking powder

3 ounces cream cheese, softened

¼ cup powdered sugar

1 to 2 tablespoons fresh orange juice

Fresh fruit, for decorating

Preheat the oven to 350°F and line a baking sheet with parchment paper.

In a small bowl, beat together the butter and sugar with an electric mixer on medium speed. Beat until light and fluffy.

Add the egg yolk and vanilla, and beat until combined.

Sprinkle the flour and baking powder on top of the mixture.

Beat until the dough comes together.

Form the dough into a ball and press it flat into a 6-inch disk on the baking sheet.

Bake for 10 to 12 minutes.

Let the cookie cool completely, leaving it on the baking sheet.

When ready to serve, beat together the cream cheese, powdered sugar, and 1 tablespoon of orange juice with an electric mixer on medium speed until light and fluffy. Add additional orange juice as needed to achieve a spreadable consistency.

Frost the cookie with the cream cheese, decorate with fresh fruit, slice, and serve.

Can I suggest something a little less expected on Valentine's Day? Sure, a warm chocolate dessert is always good (and if you're going that route, my Little Brownie Pots on page 111 are a great choice). But I think a chewy chocolate cookie stuffed with strawberry ice cream is even better. It's not Valentine's Day without chocolate and strawberries, and this fun spin on that flavor combo is all I want from my valentine! *Makes 4 sandwiches*

CHOCOLATE ICE CREAM SANDWICHES

FOR THE CHOCOLATE COOKIES:

¾ cup all-purpose flour

3 tablespoons unsweetened cocoa powder

Pinch of fine sea salt

4 tablespoons unsalted butter, softened

⅔ cup powdered sugar

2 tablespoons dark brown sugar

1¼ teaspoon vanilla extract

1 large egg yolk

2 tablespoons molasses

2 tablespoons granulated sugar, for flattening cookies

FOR SERVING:

1 pint store-bought strawberry ice cream

First, make the cookies: preheat the oven to 350°F and line a baking sheet with parchment or a silicone mat.

Whisk together the flour, cocoa, and salt. Set aside.

In a separate bowl, beat the butter, powdered sugar, brown sugar, and vanilla until fluffy.

Finally, beat in the egg yolk and molasses.

Add the dry ingredients to the wet in three batches and beat until just combined. Divide the dough in half by eye, and make four dough scoops out of each. Roll the dough in your hands to make eight balls and space them evenly on the baking sheet. Dip the bottom of a small glass in the sugar and lightly press the cookies flat.

Bake for 10 minutes.

While the cookies bake, let the ice cream soften at room temperature for about 15 minutes.

When the ice cream is soft, scoop all of it out of the carton and into an 8-inch square brownie pan. Press it as flat as possible.

When the cookies have cooled, use a 3-inch cookie or biscuit cutter (about the same size as the cookies) to cut out four perfect "slices" of ice cream.

Place each slice of ice cream between two cookies and serve immediately, or wrap in plastic wrap and freeze, then rest them on the counter 5 minutes before serving.

STRAWBERRY HAND PIES

FOR THE CRUST:

¾ cup all-purpose flour

¼ teaspoon granulated sugar

⅛ teaspoon fine sea salt

4 tablespoons cold
unsalted butter, diced

3 to 4 tablespoons ice water

FOR THE FILLING:

1 cup sliced strawberries

Pinch of lemon zest

1 tablespoon granulated sugar

1 tablespoon cornstarch

Pinch of pepper

1 egg, beaten

Coarse sugar (optional)

In a small food processor, combine all of the crust ingredients except the water.

Pulse until the butter is evenly dispersed and about the size of rice grains.

Slowly add the water, 1 tablespoon at a time, pulsing until the dough clumps together in large chunks.

Remove the dough from the food processor, wrap in plastic, and chill for 1 hour.

Preheat the oven to 375°F.

Combine the sliced strawberries, lemon zest, sugar, cornstarch, and pepper in a small bowl. Set aside.

Flour a surface and roll out the dough to about ¼-inch thick (about 8 inches wide and 4 inches across).

Use a pizza wheel to cut eight equally sized rectangles from the dough.

Place four of the dough rectangles on a baking sheet lined with parchment paper.

Divide the strawberry mixture on top of four of the rectangles.

Lightly roll out the remaining four dough pieces until they're slightly larger than the first four, and then drape them carefully on top of the strawberry-covered dough pieces. Use your fingers to pinch the edges of the dough together.

Brush the pies with the beaten egg mixture, sprinkle with coarse sugar (if using), and bake for 25 minutes.

After 25 minutes, the pies should be oozing strawberry juice. At this point, I like to turn on the broiler and crisp up the edges, but it's entirely optional. Keep an eye on the pies—they will burn in less than 1 minute under a close broiler.

There's nothing better than pie. Wait—a mini pie you can hold in your hand might be better than pie. That said, you do not have to share these pies. They're all for you.

Switch out the fruit as it comes into season: strawberries in the spring, peaches in the summer, apples in the fall, cranberries (with orange zest) or pears in the winter.

I included my easiest recipe for flaky piecrust here. But you are more than welcome to use store-bought, refrigerated pie crust, or defrosted frozen puff pastry in its place. No matter what you use, all roads lead to pie.

Makes 4 individual pies

Though hard to believe, there are times when a surplus of fresh fruit doesn't get eaten fast enough in our house. It doesn't happen often, but when it does, I always wrap the extra fruit in pastry dough and sprinkle a little sugar on top. This recipe makes two little fruit tarts. I love that you don't have to have a special baking pan to make such cute little pastries. These "tarts" are really crostatas because the dough is loosely folded around the fruit. I think it goes without saying, but please, use any kind of leftover fruit you have in your house! Any type of stone fruit (pitted, of course), fresh berries, a mix of the two—anything, really! As long as you keep the fruit to around 6 ounces total weight, you'll be fine. *Makes 2 tarts*

DIY FRUIT TARTS

FOR THE CRUST:

½ cup all-purpose flour

1 teaspoon granulated sugar

⅛ teaspoon fine sea salt

2 tablespoons cold unsalted butter, diced

2 to 3 tablespoons cold water

FOR THE FILLING:

6 ounces fresh fruit (e.g. 1 small peach, peeled and sliced + a handful of fresh blueberries)

4 teaspoons granulated sugar, plus extra for sprinkling

Zest of ½ lemon

1 large egg yolk, beaten

FOR SERVING:

2 scoops vanilla ice cream

EASY TIP: *You can substitute store-bought piecrust for the tart dough. Use a 5-inch biscuit cutter to cut out two rounds of dough from 1 sheet of piecrust.*

Preheat the oven to 375°F.

First, make the crust: combine the flour, sugar, and salt in a small bowl. With your fingertips, work the cold, diced butter into the flour mixture.

When the butter is evenly dispersed and about the size of rice grains, add 2 tablespoons of cold water to the dough. Stir until a shaggy dough forms. If there are stray bits of flour at the bottom of the bowl, or if the dough seems dry, add the remaining tablespoon of water.

Gather the dough into a ball, wrap it in plastic wrap, and press it into a flat disk.

Refrigerate the dough disk for 30 minutes.

Meanwhile, prep your fruit by washing, peeling, slicing, and/or pitting it, whatever you need to do depending on the fruit you're working with.

Combine the fruit with the 4 teaspoons of sugar and lemon zest. (No matter which fruits I use, I always include the lemon zest because I find it makes all flavors pop.) Stir to combine.

Divide the chilled dough in half and roll out two 5-inch circles.

Move each circle to a baking pan.

Evenly divide the fruit into the middle of each dough circle. Using your fingers, carefully pick up the edges of the dough and fold it over the fruit by about 1 inch. See the photo for reference.

Brush the egg yolk on the edges of the crust, sprinkle with sugar, and bake for 25 to 30 minutes.

Let the tarts cool slightly, then serve each with a scoop of vanilla ice cream on top.

TEXAS WHITE SHEET CAKE

Yes, this cake serves slightly more than two people, but it's still smaller than the average sheet cake, which serves, well, an army. I'm so happy to put our mini baking sheet to use to make a cake that serves four to six people.

I've been loyal to Texas chocolate sheet cake for years, but I've always heard great things about the white/almond version. It doesn't disappoint!

Makes 4 to 6 servings

FOR THE CAKE:

1 cup all-purpose flour

1 cup granulated sugar

⅛ teaspoon fine sea salt

8 tablespoons (1 stick) unsalted butter, melted

¾ cup buttermilk

1 large egg, beaten

½ teaspoon baking soda

½ teaspoon vanilla

½ teaspoon almond extract

FOR THE FROSTING:

7 tablespoons unsalted butter

3 tablespoons milk

½ teaspoon vanilla

¼ teaspoon almond extract

2 heaping cups powdered sugar

½ cup sliced almonds, toasted

Preheat the oven to 350°F and lightly spray a quarter-sheet pan with cooking spray.

First, make the cake: in a medium-size bowl, whisk together the flour, sugar, and salt.

In a measuring cup, stir together the melted butter, buttermilk, egg, baking soda, vanilla, and almond extract.

Add the buttermilk mixture to the flour mixture.

Stir together all cake ingredients very well and then pour into the prepared pan.

Bake cake for 15 to 18 minutes, or until an inserted toothpick comes out clean.

While the cake bakes, make the frosting. In a saucepan, melt the butter over medium-low heat.

Stir in the buttermilk and vanilla until well combined.

Remove the pan from the heat and whisk in the powdered sugar.

When the cake comes out of the oven, immediately pour the frosting over it. Use an offset spatula to spread the frosting to the edges of the pan.

Sprinkle with the sliced almonds.

Let the cake cool for at least 30 minutes before serving.

TEXAS CHOCOLATE SHEET CAKE

I couldn't resist slipping in my recipe for the chocolate version of the Texas sheet cake, just in case you need it. (You definitely need it.) *Makes 4 to 6 servings*

FOR THE CAKE:

1 cup all-purpose flour

1 cup granulated sugar

⅛ teaspoon fine sea salt

8 tablespoons (1 stick) unsalted butter

2 heaping tablespoons unsweetened cocoa powder

½ cup boiling water

¼ cup buttermilk

1 large egg, beaten

½ teaspoon baking soda

½ teaspoon vanilla

FOR THE FROSTING:

7 tablespoons unsalted butter

2 heaping tablespoons cocoa powder

3 tablespoons buttermilk

1 teaspoon vanilla

2 heaping cups powdered sugar

Preheat the oven to 350°F and lightly spray a quarter-sheet pan with cooking spray.

In a medium-size bowl, whisk together the flour, sugar, and salt.

In a small saucepan over medium-low heat, melt the butter. Once the butter has melted, stir in the cocoa powder and boiling water.

In a measuring cup, stir together the buttermilk, egg, baking soda, and vanilla.

Add the buttermilk mixture to the flour mixture, followed by the cocoa powder and boiling water mixture.

Stir together all cake ingredients very well and then pour into the prepared pan.

Bake cake for 15 to 18 minutes, or until an inserted toothpick comes out clean.

While the cake bakes, make the frosting. In the same saucepan, melt the butter over medium-low heat. Stir in the cocoa powder, buttermilk, and vanilla until well-combined. Remove the pan from the heat and whisk in the powdered sugar.

When the cake comes out of the oven, immediately pour the frosting over it. Use an offset spatula to spread the frosting to the edges of the pan.

Let the cake cool for at least 30 minutes before serving.

MIXED BERRY CROSTINI

You and I are filing this under "healthy and light" desserts, but really, no one will be thinking that as they eat them.

When the berries are appearing at your at farmers' markets (and the summer sun is beating down on your back), grab all the berries you can. Snag a whole wheat baguette and some local ricotta cheese. At home, we're going to stir some honey and orange zest into the ricotta cheese, slice up the baguette, and pile the berries on top.

This is the kind of recipe you can easily adapt to serve two or twenty. My local bread shop carries a mini whole wheat baguette that I love to buy for my daughter, but if you have a large baguette, freeze the extra slices and pull them out as needed.

I've been known to eat this dessert for breakfast, and I think you should too. *Makes 8 crostini*

8 slices (½-inch thick) whole wheat baguette

½ cup whole milk ricotta cheese

Zest of 1 orange

¼ teaspoon vanilla

1 to 2 tablespoons local honey (to taste)

1½ cups fresh fruit (cherries, berries, or a mix)

Place the slices of baguette on a small baking sheet and slide into a low oven, just to warm the slices through.

Meanwhile, stir together the ricotta, orange zest, vanilla, and honey. Taste and adjust to your own liking and sweetness level.

When the bread is just warm, remove it from the oven, slather each slice with the flavored ricotta, and top with fresh fruit.

To serve, drizzle extra honey on top so that it's messy. You can't eat dessert without getting a little messy.

MINI MOON PIES

There was supposed to be a recipe for moon pies in my first book, *Dessert for Two*. The truth is, I became so hung up on oatmeal cream pies that I skipped over moon pies. I couldn't imagine you would need another cookie sandwich stuffed with marshmallow cream. But, as it turns out, I was wrong. You can never have enough cookie sandwich recipes.

I call these "quick" moon pies, because the only thing we're making from scratch is the cookie dough. And really, it's so easy, just a small batch of shortbread dough that has honey for sweetness and crispness. The honey also lends the graham cracker–like taste that moon pies have. Once the cookies are done, we're going to spread on marshmallow cream (yes, straight from the jar!), dunk in chocolate, and then devour.

You can dunk the cookies entirely in chocolate for more authentic moon pies. The recipe accounts for plenty of extra chocolate for double dipping too! *Makes 6 mini moon pies*

FOR THE DOUGH:
4 tablespoons unsalted butter, softened

¼ cup powdered sugar

1 tablespoon honey

½ teaspoon vanilla extract

¼ teaspoon fine sea salt

½ cup all-purpose flour, plus extra for rolling

FOR ASSEMBLING MOON PIES:
About ¼ cup marshmallow fluff

1 cup chocolate chips

1 tablespoon coconut oil

Preheat the oven to 350°F and line a baking sheet with parchment paper (or spray very well with cooking spray).

In a medium-size bowl, add the butter, powdered sugar, honey, and vanilla. Beat the mixture on medium speed with an electric mixer until light and fluffy.

Next, sprinkle the flour and salt evenly on top. Beat together until just combined.

If the mixture seems overly soft, like cake frosting, place it in the fridge for 30 minutes to chill. (The first time you make this recipe, it's not a bad idea to chill it.)

Next, heavily flour a board. Place the cookie dough on top and sprinkle more flour on top of the dough. Use your fingers to press the dough out into a rough 6-inch square, using lots of flour as you go.

Using a 2-inch-wide biscuit cutter, cut out 12 circles from the dough. Hopefully, the dough will pop out of the cutter easily or slide off the cutting board. If not, use a spatula to carefully move the dough circles to the baking sheet.

Bake for 10 minutes, or until the edges of the cookies start to turn golden brown.

Let cookies cool completely, leaving them on the baking sheet.

Meanwhile, melt the chocolate chips and coconut oil in a double boiler. Alternatively, set a microwave to 50 percent power and heat the chocolate chips and coconut oil in 30-second pulses, stirring between each pulse, until melted and smooth.

Spread a scant teaspoon of marshmallow filling on top of six cookies. Press the remaining cookies on top, dunk in the melted chocolate, and place on a wax paper-lined plate to chill in the fridge for a few minutes before serving.

These cookies keep in the fridge for a few days or tightly wrapped in the freezer for your next moon pie craving. The longer the sandwiches sit, the softer the cookies become (and more authentic to the original moon pies too!).

CLASSIC
>>·>> · <<·<<
LOAF
PAN

SALTED CARAMEL BARS

I say you start here with this recipe. It's calling your name, I just know it. Buttery rich shortbread sandwiched by salted caramel. It doesn't get much better than this.

   I'm going to give you my recipe for salted caramel sauce, but a jarred version is totally fine here. My recipe makes 1 cup of caramel sauce, and you'll only need ¼ cup, plus a little extra for drizzling, to make these bars. While I'm normally averse to leftover dessert, I make an exception for salted caramel sauce. Put it in a jar in the fridge, and you'll find plenty of things to use it in throughout the week. *Makes 2 generous servings*

FOR THE BARS:

7 tablespoons unsalted butter, at room temperature

¼ cup powdered sugar

¾ cup + 1 tablespoon all-purpose flour

⅛ teaspoon fine sea salt

¼ cup salted caramel sauce (recipe follows, or use store-bought), plus extra for drizzling

MAKE THE BARS:

Preheat the oven to 350°F.

Line a bread loaf pan with parchment paper, making sure to leave enough excess to make handles to help you move it out of the pan.

In a small bowl, combine the butter, powdered sugar, flour, and salt. Using a pastry blender, two knives, or simply your fingers, blend the butter into the flour mixture until a soft, crumbly dough forms.

Press three-quarters of the dough onto the bottom of the loaf pan and press it flat.

Spread ¼ cup of caramel sauce on top.

Dot the remaining dough over the top of the caramel sauce, focusing on the edges.

Bake for 30 minutes.

Let the bars cool slightly, then lift them out of the pan to cool completely.

Before serving, drizzle extra caramel sauce on top, if desired (it's very desirable.)

FOR THE SALTED CARAMEL SAUCE:

1 cup granulated sugar

¼ cup water

½ cup + 2 tablespoons half-and-half (or cream)

1 tablespoon unsalted butter

1 teaspoon fine sea salt

1 teaspoon pure vanilla

MAKE THE CARAMEL SAUCE, IF USING:

In a deep saucepan (at least 2 quarts—no smaller, because the mixture bubbles up!), add the sugar and water. Whisk to combine.

Turn the heat to medium-high and let the sugar melt and dissolve without stirring. If you see sugar crystals on the sides of the pan, use a pastry brush dipped in water to gently push them back in the pan. Do not stir.

Once the sugar is dissolved, crank the heat to high and watch it turn an amber color. Watch closely, it happens quickly! You can swirl the pan gently to evenly brown the caramel.

Meanwhile, heat the half-and-half (or cream) until it's steaming and small bubbles are forming around the edges.

Turn off the heat to the sugar mixture and add the half-and-half all at once. Be careful—it bubbles up triple the size! It is very hot!

Next, whisk in the butter, salt, and vanilla. Whisk until smooth. Pour the mixture into a jar to cool and use as you like.

ANGEL FOOD JAM CAKE

So, maybe an angel food cake baked in a loaf pan serves slightly more than two people, but still, it's less than the standard angel food tube pan recipes. I'd say you could get seven or eight slices out of this loaf. I lost count because I started eating while I was slicing . . . *Makes 2 generous servings*

¾ cup granulated sugar, divided

½ cup all-purpose flour

1 tablespoon cornstarch

7 large egg whites

2 teaspoons vanilla extract

¾ teaspoon cream of tartar

¼ teaspoon fine sea salt

6 tablespoons raspberry jam

Fresh raspberries, for garnish

Fresh whipped cream, for garnish

Preheat the oven to 325°F and have a loaf pan ready. Ensure it's not a nonstick pan, and do not grease it in any way.

In a small bowl, whisk together ¼ cup of the sugar, flour, and cornstarch. Set aside.

To the bowl of a stand mixer, add the egg whites, vanilla, cream of tartar, and salt. Beat on medium speed until foamy, about 30 seconds. Slowly stream in the remaining ½ cup of sugar, one tablespoon at a time, while beating. Continue to beat on high speed until soft, floppy peaks form, about 4 minutes.

Next, add one-third of the dry ingredients and fold in using a spatula. Proper folding technique is down the middle and around the sides, or the over-under method. Your goal is to incorporate everything without deflating all the air you just whipped into the egg whites. Repeat with the remaining flour mixture in two increments. Take your time, go slow—it will take the better part of 5 minutes to fold in the flour mixture and ensure no lumps remain.

Pour the batter into the loaf pan. Place the loaf pan on a baking sheet and bake for 38 to 42 minutes. The cake is done when the top is no longer sticky to the touch and the cracks in the cake are not sticky either.

Once the cake comes out of the oven, immediately invert it over two cans. The cake should dry upside down to prevent deflation. Let the cake cool for 60 minutes.

Once the cake is cool, run a knife around the edges of the pan and gently let the cake fall out onto a cutting board. With the cake on its side, use a serrated knife (an electric carving knife is even better) and slice the cake horizontally into three even layers. (See photo for reference.)

Place two layers of plastic wrap that are more than triple the size of the cake on a clean surface. Place the bottom layer of the cake in the middle of the plastic wrap and spread with 3 tablespoons of the jam. Place the second layer on top, followed by the remaining 3 tablespoons of the jam. Finally, add the top layer on the cake and wrap the cake tightly in plastic wrap. Press the cake gently to make it stick together, then place it back in the pan you baked it in. Refrigerate for 4 hours to help the layers set together.

Slice the cake and serve with raspberries and whipped cream.

CHEESECAKE
IN A LOAF PAN

I'm having the hardest time deciding the serving size of this small cheese-cake made in a loaf pan. I think just how much cheesecake you can eat is personal. A personal accomplishment, if you ask me, but nevertheless, the answer varies.

The way I slice it into little triangles, you will get five smaller-than-average slices of cheesecake. Can you eat two? Can you eat three? Or do you serve this at a dinner party and give each guest one small slice? I've done all three.

Keep this small cheesecake recipe in your back pocket. You'll need it more than you think. *Makes 2 generous servings*

FOR THE CRUST:

8 graham cracker sheets

2 tablespoons unsalted butter, melted

1 tablespoon granulated sugar

FOR THE FILLING:

2 (8-ounce) packages of cream cheese, at room temperature

½ cup granulated sugar

1 large egg, beaten

1 teaspoon vanilla extract

1 teaspoon fresh lemon juice

1 (21-ounce) can cherry pie filling, for serving (optional)

4 ounces chopped chocolate and 2 teaspoons coconut oil, for serving (optional)

Preheat the oven to 325°F and line a loaf pan with parchment paper. It doesn't have to cover every side—just the two longest sides.

In a small food processor (or plastic zip-top bag), crush the graham crackers into crumbs. Add the melted butter and sugar, and stir/mix until combined.

Press the crumbs into the loaf pan and bake for 25 minutes until lightly golden brown.

Meanwhile, beat together the cream cheese and sugar with an electric mixer on medium speed until light and fluffy. Beat in the egg, followed by the vanilla and lemon juice.

Pour the cheesecake mixture over the crust.

Lower the oven to 300°F and bake the cheesecake for 30 to 40 minutes, until the entire surface is set and not sticky. It will have a slightly golden yellow hue. An inserted toothpick should not come out wet with batter.

EASY TIP: *Use the rest of the can of cherries to make the cheesecake dip in the Ramekins chapter.*

Let the cheesecake cool near the oven (drastic temperature changes cause cracks in cheesecake). Once fully cooled, move to the refrigerator for at least 4 hours. Place the can of cherries in the fridge with the cheesecake if using.

If serving with chocolate, melt the chocolate and coconut oil in a double boiler. Alternatively, set a microwave to 50 percent power and heat the chocolate and coconut oil in 30-second pulses, stirring between each pulse, until melted and smooth.

Top with cherries or chocolate (or both—the world is your oyster!) before serving.

CHOCOLATE CHERRY COCONUT BARS

Sometimes cookie bars can be uneventful. Yes, it's a cookie. In bar form. Big deal.

But those who have tasted *these* cookie bars keep insisting to me that they are, in fact, a big deal. A huge deal.

Chocolate chunks, canned cherries (but never the bright red ones), and coconut love to be wrapped in dough. The flavors go together so well, and they will become a big deal in your life. *Makes 2 generous servings*

3 tablespoons
unsalted butter, melted

½ cup brown sugar

1 large egg yolk

½ teaspoon vanilla

¼ teaspoon almond extract

Pinch of fine sea salt

½ cup all-purpose flour

¼ teaspoon baking powder

¼ cup chocolate chips

¼ cup coconut shreds (sweet or unsweet, your choice)

¼ cup diced canned cherries (I use Morello cherries)

Preheat the oven to 350°F and line a loaf pan with enough parchment paper to overhang the sides and make handles for lifting the blondies out.

In a medium-size bowl, stir together the melted butter and brown sugar with a wooden spoon until well blended.

Stir in the egg yolk, vanilla, almond extract, and salt.

Sprinkle the flour and baking powder evenly on top and stir it together.

Finally, stir in the chocolate chips, coconut, and cherries.

Bake for 20 to 24 minutes. Use a toothpick to test for doneness—you don't want the toothpick to come out dry; some moist crumbs clinging is what you're looking for. Immediately lift the blondies out of the pan and allow to cool completely on a wire rack before devouring.

BEST EVER FROSTED BROWNIES

If you're new to my *Dessert for Two* universe, let's bring you up to speed real quick: I make a lot of desserts in bread loaf pans. The standard 9-inch loaf pan is perfect for making two servings of brownies and bars.

When you bake these incredible brownies, you just slice them in half and share.

These brownies somehow manage to be both cakey and fudgy at the same time, so no matter which brownie camp you are in, you're going to love these! *Makes 2 generous servings*

FOR THE BROWNIES:
8 tablespoons (1 stick) unsalted butter

½ cup cocoa powder

1 cup + 2 tablespoons granulated sugar

1 teaspoon vanilla extract

¼ teaspoon fine sea salt

1 large egg

½ cup all-purpose flour

FOR THE FROSTING:
6 tablespoons unsalted butter, softened

¼ cup cocoa powder

¾ cup powdered sugar

2 to 3 tablespoons milk or cream

Preheat the oven to 325°F and line a 9-inch bread loaf pan with parchment paper.

In a microwave-safe bowl, combine the butter, cocoa powder, and sugar. Microwave at full power for 30 seconds. Stir the mixture and return it to the microwave for another 30 seconds. Stir again. Add one more 30-second pulse if the butter isn't mostly melted.

Let the mixture cool for 1 minute.

Stir in the vanilla and salt.

Stir in the egg.

Finally, add the flour and stir vigorously for about 1 minute, or 50 strokes.

Scrape the mixture into the loaf pan and bake for about 40 minutes. The top of the brownie surface should appear dry and be starting to crack. Do not overbake because you want the inside to be fudgy.

Meanwhile, beat together all of the frosting ingredients, adding milk or cream as needed to make the frosting spreadable.

Frost the brownies once cool and cut in half to serve.

EASIEST RICE CRISPY TREATS

First, brownies in the microwave. Now? Rice crispy treats in the microwave.
Makes 2 generous servings

1 tablespoon unsalted butter

1 cup (packed) mini marshmallows

2 cups crispy rice cereal

Pinch of fine sea salt

Place the butter in a microwave-safe bowl. Melt in the microwave at full power, about 15 seconds.

Next, add the marshmallows and microwave for about 25 seconds, until the marshmallows melt.

Stir the butter and marshmallows together very well.

Add the pinch of salt and the cereal all at once.

Stir, stir, stir.

Using wax paper, press the mixture into a bread loaf pan to shape it into a loaf.

Slice in half and serve.

S'MORES RICE CRISPY TREATS

I mean, why shouldn't we take our regular rice crispy treats, stir in chocolate, pour them over graham crackers, and top them with torched marshmallows? It's too easy and delicious not to! *Makes 2 generous servings*

2 graham cracker sheets

1 tablespoon unsalted butter

1 cup (packed) mini marshmallows

2 cups crispy rice cereal

Pinch of fine sea salt

⅓ cup chopped chocolate (or chocolate chips)

9 large marshmallows

First, line a bread loaf pan with the graham crackers, breaking them up to fit as needed.

Place the butter in a microwave-safe bowl. Melt in the microwave at full power, about 15 seconds.

Next, add the marshmallows and microwave for about 25 seconds, until the marshmallows melt.

Stir the butter and marshmallows together very well.

Add the pinch of salt and the cereal all at once.

Stir, stir, stir.

Using wax paper, press the mixture into a bread loaf pan to shape it into a loaf.

Sprinkle the chocolate on top of the mixture while everything's warm and press gently to adhere the chocolate.

Snip the marshmallows in half with kitchen scissors and evenly distribute them over the top. Use a kitchen torch to lightly toast the marshmallows.

Slice in half and serve.

Another day, another chance to grab the box of extra-dark cocoa powder from the pantry. In fact, I have completely made the switch to dark cocoa powder when it comes to chocolate frostings.

Oh, I'm sorry, did you come here for cake too? We should really talk about this banana cake. A friend recently gushed to me about her mom's banana cake with chocolate frosting. And it got me thinking: Can banana cake really be that much different than banana bread? The answer is maybe it can, but it's also okay to not stray too far either. Banana bread is soft, tender, and delicious. And banana cake is also all of those things, but with a dark chocolate peanut butter frosting. You feel me? *Makes 2 generous servings*

BANANA CAKE + CHOCOLATE PEANUT BUTTER FROSTING

FOR THE CAKE:

1 large banana, smushed

6 tablespoons granulated sugar

1 large egg

2 tablespoons neutral oil (or coconut oil)

¾ teaspoon vanilla extract

¼ cup sour cream

¾ cup all-purpose flour

¼ teaspoon cinnamon

⅛ teaspoon fine sea salt

¼ teaspoon baking soda

½ teaspoon baking powder

FOR THE FROSTING:

1½ tablespoons unsalted butter, at room temperature

2 tablespoons peanut butter

1½ tablespoons dark cocoa powder

1 cup powdered sugar

½ teaspoon vanilla extract

A few splashes of milk, as needed

Preheat the oven to 375°F and line a bread loaf pan with parchment paper. (I use parchment paper to line all of the pan, with some extra paper on the edges to use as handles to lift out the dessert.)

In a medium-size bowl, smash the banana very well until almost no lumps remain.

Next, stir in the sugar, egg, oil, and vanilla extract. Stir very well until blended.

Add the sour cream and stir until evenly incorporated.

In a separate small bowl, whisk together the flour, cinnamon, salt, baking soda, and baking powder.

Add the dry ingredients to the bowl of wet ingredients and stir until combined.

Pour the batter into the loaf pan and bake for 28 to 32 minutes, or until a toothpick comes out mostly clean, with a few moist crumbs clinging to it.

Let the cake cool on a wire rack

Meanwhile, beat together all of the frosting ingredients until light and fluffy, adding milk as needed to make a smooth, spreadable consistency.

Frost the cake with the chocolate peanut butter frosting and serve sliced in half, for two large pieces of banana cake.

BEER BROWNIES

Another excellent contender for a Valentine's Day gift or dessert! While these are a tad more work than regular brownies, boiling beer on the stove until it reduces to a syrup is the best flavor enhancement possible for warm, chocolatey brownies. You'll use the beer syrup in the brownies and a little in the frosting too. Only use the optional unsweetened chocolate if you like fudgy brownies; omit it if you prefer more cake-y brownies.

Makes 2 generous servings

FOR THE BEER BROWNIES:

1 cup dark beer
(I used coffee stout)

8 tablespoons (1 stick) unsalted butter

½ cup + 1 tablespoon unsweetened cocoa powder

1 cup + 2 tablespoons granulated sugar

2 ounces unsweetened chocolate, chopped (optional)

1 large egg white

1 teaspoon vanilla extract

¼ teaspoon fine sea salt

½ cup all-purpose flour

FOR THE FROSTING:

6 tablespoons unsalted butter, softened

1 cup powdered sugar

First, make the beer concentrate: Add the beer to a small saucepan and boil until it reduces to ⅓ cup. It will take about 20 minutes. Keep an eye on it to prevent it from boiling over.

Preheat the oven to 325°F and line a loaf pan with parchment paper.

In a microwave-safe bowl, combine the butter, cocoa powder, sugar, and unsweetened chocolate (if using). Microwave at full power for 30 seconds. Stir, then microwave for another 30 seconds. Let the mixture cool for 1 minute.

Stir in 4 tablespoons of the beer concentrate, the egg white, vanilla, and salt.

Finally, mix in the flour and stir for 50 strokes to incorporate and activate the gluten in the flour.

Pour the mixture into the loaf pan and bake for 40 to 45 minutes. It's done when the surface is dry and an inserted toothpick has only moist crumbs sticking to it. Let cool.

Once the brownies are cool, make the frosting: beat together the softened butter and powdered sugar until combined.

Beat in the remaining beer concentrate (1 tablespoon).

Frost the brownies and serve.

CHAI BARS

You probably know by now how much of a tea lover I am; from the Lemon Matcha Cake Roll (page 181) to the Earl Grey Crème Brûlée (page 123) that I crave all day, there's hardly a way that I haven't crammed tea into my desserts.

These gooey chai bars are my favorite chai-flavored dessert (until I make the next one), but if you lack all of these spices, go ahead and make it just with cinnamon (1½ teaspoons total). You'll still get a warm, gooey spice bar that tastes best first thing in the morning. *Makes 2 generous servings*

FOR THE BARS:

¼ teaspoon ground ginger

½ teaspoon ground cardamom

¼ teaspoon freshly ground black pepper

¼ teaspoon ground cloves

½ teaspoon ground cinnamon

1 cup all-purpose flour

½ teaspoon baking powder

⅛ teaspoon baking soda

5⅓ tablespoons unsalted butter, melted

1 cup brown sugar

1 large egg

¾ teaspoon vanilla extract

FOR THE TOPPING:

½ reserved teaspoon of the spice mixture (from above)

⅛ cup granulated sugar

½ tablespoon unsalted butter, melted

Preheat the oven to 350°F and line a loaf pan with parchment paper or foil to prevent sticking.

Combine all of the spices together in a small bowl and set aside.

Next, whisk together the flour, all of the spices except ½ teaspoon (reserve it for topping after baking), baking powder, and baking soda.

In a separate bowl, whisk together the melted butter, brown sugar, eggs, and vanilla.

Stir the wet ingredients into the dry until no streaks of flour remain.

Pour the batter into the prepared pan and bake for 20 minutes.

Start testing the bars at 17 minutes—you want them to bake but still be soft in the center. Wet crumbs clinging to the toothpick are okay, but the top should be dry to the touch.

While the bars are still warm, make the topping: Melt the butter. Stir the granulated sugar and reserved spice mixture into the butter and brush on the bars.

Let cool, slice, and serve.

PEANUT BUTTER BARS

The name—peanut butter bars—sounds normal, but the flavor is very unique here. This might be the only time you've seen peanut butter without its other half, chocolate. It's rare for me to keep the two apart. (Please tell me I'm not the only one who dips a spoon in peanut butter and rolls it in mini chocolate chips as an afternoon snack!)

But when it comes to these bars, think of them like a lemon bar . . . but with peanut butter! It's different than anything you've ever had before, but I'm a big fan of widening your dessert horizons. And your pant size.

Makes 2 generous servings

7 tablespoons unsalted butter, at room temperature

¼ cup powdered sugar, plus extra for serving

¾ cup + 1 tablespoon + ¼ cup all-purpose flour

½ teaspoon fine sea salt, divided

¼ cup peanut butter

½ cup + 2 tablespoons granulated sugar

2 large eggs

Preheat the oven to 350°F and line a loaf pan with parchment paper, leaving excess paper for handles to remove the bars.

In a medium-size bowl, stir together the butter, powdered sugar, ¾ cups plus 1 tablespoon of the flour, and ¼ teaspoon salt using a spatula.

Press the dough evenly into the bottom of the loaf pan and bake for 20 minutes, until lightly golden brown on the edges. Don't be afraid of a little color.

Meanwhile, wipe out the bowl and use it to beat together the remaining ingredients: peanut butter, remaining ¼ cup flour, granulated sugar, eggs, and remaining ¼ teaspoon salt. Beat with an electric mixer until light and fluffy, about 45 seconds.

When the crust is done, pour the peanut butter mixture on top and return it to the oven for 20 to 25 minutes, until the top is dry and starting to crackle.

Cool the bars in the pan for 5 minutes, then remove using the parchment handles.

Slice in half and serve with extra powdered sugar sprinkled on top.

PECAN PIE CARAMELITAS

Caramelitas may look unassuming, like they're just another cookie bar. They are not. They are the best cookie bar. The one, the only.

It's essentially cookie dough stuffed with caramel and punctuated with pecans and chocolate chunks. The flavor combination is incredible.

I recommend chilling them overnight for easy slicing, but it can be so hard to wait! *Makes 2 generous servings*

½ cup + 2 tablespoons all-purpose flour

5 tablespoons quick oats (you can pulse rolled oats in a food processor a few times for similar results)

¼ cup dark brown sugar

Pinch of fine sea salt

7 tablespoons cold unsalted butter, diced

¼ cup chopped pecans

⅓ cup chocolate chunks

⅓ cup store-bought caramel sauce

Preheat the oven to 350°F and line a loaf pan with parchment paper (do not use foil). Spray the parchment paper with cooking spray. These bars are very sticky! Be sure to leave enough parchment overhanging the pan to use as handles to get the bars out of the pan.

In a small bowl, mix together the flour, oats, brown sugar, and salt.

Add the butter to the flour mixture and work it though the dough using two knives or a pastry blender. The dough will be similar to cookie dough.

Divide the dough in half.

Press half of the dough into the baking pan.

Sprinkle the pecans and chocolate chunks on top.

Evenly drizzle the caramel sauce on top.

Scatter the remaining dough on top. It won't completely cover the caramel and nuts.

Bake for 25 minutes, until the caramel is bubbling and the crust is starting to brown.

Let cool completely before removing from the pan.

Slice in half and serve. (They're even easier to slice if chilled first.)

PECAN PIE BARS

Pecan pie is an oddity in my house, despite my house being firmly rooted in Southern soil. The thing is, my brother has a horrible allergy to pecans. One of his sweet babies has peanut allergies, too. So, nuts are just not something that we throw around too often. However, every year for Thanksgiving, my Dad makes a pecan pie. We all feel a little guilty eating it in front of my brother, but there's always pumpkin pie, apple crisp, and chocolate cake for him to choose from. You didn't think we would make only one dessert on a holiday, did you?

I scaled down my favorite pecan pie bar recipe to make in a loaf pan, and it's a very good thing these babies are small-batch. I can't get enough of the crisp shortbread crust, gooey sweet center, and toasted pecans. Every bite, though laden with guilt, is so very worth it. *Makes 2 generous servings*

FOR THE CRUST:

4 tablespoons unsalted butter, at room temperature

3 tablespoons dark brown sugar

1 cup all-purpose flour

¼ teaspoon fine sea salt

FOR THE FILLING:

2 tablespoons unsalted butter

¼ cup + 1 tablespoon brown sugar

1 tablespoon honey

1 tablespoon cream

½ cup whole pecan halves

Preheat the oven to 350 and line a loaf pan with parchment paper, leaving excess paper on the sides to use as handles for lifting the bars out.

In a small bowl, combine the butter, brown sugar, flour, and salt. Rub the butter into the flour using your fingertips or a pastry blender. The mixture should be sandy but still clump together when squeezed in your hands.

Pack the crust into the bottom of the loaf pan and bake for 20 minutes, or until the edges start to turn golden brown.

Meanwhile, combine all of the filling ingredients except the pecans in a 2-quart sauce pan. Bring this mixture to a rolling boil and boil for 1 minute. (A rolling boil is when bubbles rapidly rise to the surface across the entire surface of the mixture. Don't start timing until this happens.)

Remove the pan from the heat and stir in the pecans.

Spread the pecan mixture across the crust and return to the oven for another 20 minutes.

Let the bars cool completely in the pan (overnight is best) for easy removal and slicing.

This recipe is really a two-in-one deal. If you make the recipe and place it in the fridge, it's vanilla pudding. If you make it and pour it in an ice cream maker, it's—you guessed it!—vanilla ice cream.

I want you to go wild with the stir-ins. Try figs (soaked in honey—see my panna cotta recipe on page 143), mini chocolate chips, chopped nuts— anything you like and love! If you're going to add fruit, can I recommend a honey soak or a quick sauté in sugar in a pan? This will prevent the fruit from turning into icy rocks in the mixture. Along those same lines, any extract is welcome here—vanilla, orange, mint, etc. Taste the custard before churning so you'll know if you have something you love. *Makes 1 pint*

BASIC VANILLA ICE CREAM

1¾ cup whole milk

½ cup heavy cream

2 large egg yolks

½ cup granulated sugar

2 tablespoons cornstarch

½ teaspoon vanilla extract

Mix-ins: ½ cup softened fruit, ¼ cup chopped anything (nuts, chocolate chips, etc.)

In a 2-quart saucepan, warm the milk and heavy cream.

In a small bowl, whisk together the egg yolks, sugar, and cornstarch. At first the mixture will seem crumbly, but with 1 minute of vigorous whisking, it will lighten in color and become liquid.

Once the milk and cream mixture has small bubbles on the edges (do not let it boil!), ladle a few tablespoons into the egg mixture while constantly whisking. Do this three or four more times to temper the eggs.

Then pour everything back into the same saucepan and, stirring constantly, bring to a gentle boil—when you see the first bubbles coming to the surface, remove it from the heat and stir in the vanilla.

At this point, taste the mixture and make sure you're happy with the base flavor. Cover and chill for at least 4 hours.

Then pour the mixture into your ice-cream maker and freeze according to the manufacturer's instructions.

When the mixture looks like soft serve (mine takes 45 minutes), stir in the fruit, nuts, and any other mix-ins.

Scrape the mixture from the ice-cream maker into a loaf pan, cover, and freeze until firm. Let soften for 5 minutes before scooping and serving.

VEGAN CHOCOLATE SORBET

I just think everyone needs a chocolate ice-cream recipe in their arsenal. It just so happens that this one is vegan, and though not entirely intentional, the flavors in the chocolate shine through with a dairy-free ice cream base. You probably have to try it to believe me. But that's okay.

I based this recipe off Ina Garten's recipe for chocolate sorbet, so I knew it was a winner. I stir in fresh raspberries right before serving instead of while the ice cream is churning so that they stay soft. Fresh berries have a tendency to turn into icy rocks once they hang out in the freezer.

Another optional stir-in? Shaved dark chocolate pieces. (As many as humanly possible.) *Makes 1 pint*

1 cup granulated sugar

½ cup cocoa powder

¼ teaspoon vanilla extract

⅛ teaspoon kosher salt

1 heaping teaspoon instant espresso powder

2¼ cups water

1 tablespoon dark rum

A handful of fresh raspberries

Combine all ingredients except the rum and raspberries in a saucepan. Turn the heat to medium and stir until the sugar dissolves.

Remove from the heat and stir in the rum. Cover and chill the mixture at least 4 hours, or until very cold.

Pour the mixture in an ice-cream maker and churn according to the manufacturer's instructions.

Place the fresh-churned ice cream in a loaf pan and freeze until firm, about 2 hours.

Just before scooping and serving, smash in the fresh raspberries.

MUFFIN PAN

One-Bowl Chocolate
Cupcakes
+ Easiest Chocolate Frosting
80

One-Bowl Lemon
Cupcakes
*+ Lemon Cream
Cheese Frosting*
84

One-Bowl Vanilla
Bean Cupcakes
+ Vanilla Buttercream
85

Pumpkin Chocolate
Cupcakes
+ Vanilla Bean Buttercream
87

Perfect Homemade
Sprinkles Cupcakes
90

Marshmallow-Filled
Cupcakes
93

Peppermint Brownie Bites
94

Mini Raspberry Pies
97

Chocolate Fruit Bark
98

Mini Chocolate
Pound Cakes
with Raspberry Sauce
101

Camille's Cupcakes
*Maple Syrup Cupcakes +
Coconut Whip*
103

Olive Oil Cakelets
105

ONE-BOWL CHOCOLATE CUPCAKES + Easiest Chocolate Frosting

You know how I'm your girl? I'm your girl because I'm here for you when you have a cupcake craving. You want cupcakes, but you don't want two dozen of them, right? (Well, want and need are two very different things in life, aren't they?) All of these cupcake recipes make just four cupcakes. You can share the other two, if you want, but you really don't have to. I won't tell a soul.

Let's bake one-bowl chocolate cupcakes first. I have a feeling your cupcake craving involves chocolate. I have played with recipes for chocolate cupcakes for years, and this is, hands down, the winner. You can make them even if you don't have an egg in your fridge! I didn't intend to make eggless chocolate cupcakes, but I've found that the combination of ingredients below lets the chocolate flavor shine.

And just when you didn't think it could get better, I'll tell you my one-ingredient, easy chocolate frosting secret: a jar of chocolate hazelnut spread! It's the perfect consistency for frosting cupcakes (and the perfect flavor too!).

Makes 4 cupcakes

FOR THE CUPCAKES:

⅓ cup all-purpose flour

2 tablespoons (slightly heaped) unsweetened cocoa powder

¼ teaspoon baking soda

¼ teaspoon baking powder

¼ teaspoon instant coffee or espresso powder (optional)

⅓ cup buttermilk (or milk with ½ teaspoon vinegar added)

4 teaspoons canola oil

½ teaspoon vanilla extract

¼ cup dark brown sugar, packed

FOR THE FROSTING:

½ cup chocolate hazelnut spread

Preheat the oven to 350°F and line four cups in a muffin pan with paper liners.

In a medium-size bowl, whisk together the flour, cocoa powder, baking soda, baking powder, and instant coffee (if using).

Next, add all remaining ingredients and whisk until well combined.

Divide the batter between the paper liners, and bake for 15 to 17 minutes, until the top springs back when lightly pressed. If you underbake them, they sink slightly, so be sure to test them with a toothpick too. (But, hey, if they sink, just fill them with more chocolate hazelnut spread—it's fine!)

Let the cupcakes cool as long as humanly possible, and then frost with chocolate hazelnut spread.

ONE-BOWL LEMON CUPCAKES + Lemon Cream Cheese Frosting

In a world full of chocolate, I am a lemon dessert girl. I'm so sorry, but it's true. These lemon cupcakes are my lemon dream come true—the cake is laced with lemon zest, lemon juice, and lemon extract, and the frosting is lemon cream cheese. Pucker up, baby! *Makes 4 cupcakes*

FOR THE CUPCAKES:

4 tablespoons
unsalted butter, softened

¼ cup granulated sugar

Zest of 1 whole lemon

1 large egg white

½ teaspoon lemon extract (optional)

2 tablespoons sour cream

2 teaspoons fresh lemon juice

6 tablespoons all-purpose flour

½ teaspoon baking soda

Pinch of fine sea salt

FOR THE FROSTING:

4 ounces cream cheese, softened

3 tablespoons butter, softened

7 tablespoons powdered sugar

Juice of ½ lemon

Preheat the oven to 400°F and line four cups in a muffin pan with paper liners.

In a medium-size bowl, with an electric mixer on medium speed, beat together the butter, sugar, and lemon zest until light and fluffy, about 30 seconds.

Add the egg white and lemon extract (if using), and beat until combined. Beat in the sour cream and lemon juice.

Next, sprinkle the flour, baking soda, and salt evenly over the batter and beat on low speed until it comes together, being careful not to overmix.

Divide the batter among the paper liners and bake for 16 to 19 minutes, until the top springs back when lightly pressed. If you underbake them, they sink slightly, so be sure to test them with a toothpick too.

Let the cupcakes cool.

Beat together all frosting ingredients with a hand mixer on high speed until light and fluffy.

Frost the cupcakes and serve.

ONE-BOWL VANILLA BEAN CUPCAKES
+ Vanilla Buttercream

My mainstay. My go-to comfort: vanilla cupcakes piled with vanilla bean buttercream. *Makes 4 cupcakes*

FOR THE CUPCAKES:

4 tablespoons
unsalted butter, softened

¼ cup granulated sugar

½ of a vanilla bean, scraped

1 large egg white

2 tablespoons sour cream

6 tablespoons all-purpose flour

½ teaspoon baking soda

Pinch of fine sea salt

FOR THE FROSTING:

3 tablespoons unsalted butter

1¼ cups powdered sugar

¼ of a vanilla bean
(or 2 teaspoons extract)

Pinch of fine sea salt

1 tablespoon milk or cream

Preheat the oven to 400°F and line four cups in a muffin pan with paper liners.

In a medium-size bowl, with an electric mixer on medium speed, beat together the butter, sugar, and vanilla bean until light and fluffy, about 30 seconds.

Add the egg white and beat until combined.

Beat in the sour cream.

Next, sprinkle the flour, baking soda, and salt evenly over the batter and beat on low speed until it comes together, being careful not to overmix.

Divide the batter between the paper liners and bake for 16 to 19 minutes, until the top springs back when lightly pressed. If you underbake them, they sink slightly, so be sure to test them with a toothpick too.

Let the cupcakes cool.

To make the frosting: Beat the butter until light and fluffy, about 1 minute. Slowly add the powdered sugar, vanilla bean, and salt while continuously beating.

Add the cream, starting with just 1 tablespoon, and add more if needed to make the perfect frosting consistency.

Frost the cupcakes with the vanilla bean frosting and serve.

PUMPKIN CHOCOLATE CUPCAKES + Vanilla Bean Buttercream

If you'll allow me to say it, I will: Pumpkin can be so overdone. Pumpkin spice everything. We drink pumpkin spice lattes, we eat pumpkin spice cupcakes, and we now burn pumpkin spice candles. It's just a lot, you know? I grew tired of pumpkin and boycotted it for an entire year. Yes, I eventually missed it, but when I let it back into my life, I added chocolate. Pumpkin and chocolate is a flavor combo I could never get tired of.

To make these pretty layered cupcakes, you're going to make two batters side by side in separate bowls. The batters will share an egg. When you're ready to bake, layer them in the pan in four layers, starting with the pumpkin batter.

If you skip over the vanilla bean buttercream that tastes like the inside of an Oreo cookie, well, that's your mistake in life. *Makes 6 cupcakes*

FOR THE CHOCOLATE BATTER:

⅓ cup all-purpose flour

2 tablespoons cocoa powder

¼ teaspoon baking soda

¼ teaspoon instant espresso powder

4 teaspoons neutral-flavored oil (like grapeseed or canola)

½ teaspoon vanilla extract

¼ cup packed brown sugar

⅓ cup buttermilk

1 large egg yolk

Preheat the oven to 350°F and line six cups in a muffin pan with liners.

TO MAKE THE CHOCOLATE BATTER:
Whisk together the flour, cocoa powder, baking soda, and espresso powder. Set aside.

Whisk together the oil, vanilla, brown sugar, buttermilk, and egg yolk. Set aside.

(continued)

7 tablespoons all-purpose flour

½ teaspoon baking powder

⅛ teaspoon baking soda

¼ teaspoon fine sea salt

½ teaspoon cinnamon

¼ teaspoon freshly grated nutmeg

¼ teaspoon ground ginger

1 large egg white

½ cup canned pumpkin purée

¼ cup packed brown sugar

3 tablespoons neutral-flavored oil

3 tablespoons granulated sugar

FOR THE VANILLA BEAN BUTTERCREAM:

4 tablespoons
unsalted butter, softened

1½ cups powdered sugar

½ vanilla bean, scraped

¼ teaspoon vanilla extract

Pinch of fine sea salt

1 to 2 tablespoons heavy cream

TO MAKE THE PUMPKIN SPICE BATTER:

Whisk together the flour, baking powder, baking soda, salt, and spices. Set aside.

Whisk together the egg white, pumpkin, brown sugar, oil, and granulated sugar. Set aside.

When ready to fill the pan, mix together the dry and wet ingredients for the chocolate cupcakes. Then mix together the dry and wet ingredients for the pumpkin cupcakes. Now you have two separate batters to work with.

Layer the batters in the cupcake liners, swirling if you like. I did a layer of pumpkin on the bottom, followed by chocolate batter, pumpkin, and finally chocolate. The baking soda in the chocolate batter will make it rise up around the slightly denser pumpkin batter. Lovely!

Bake the cupcakes for 17 to 20 minutes, or until an inserted toothpick comes out with only moist crumbs.

Let the cupcakes cool in the pan for 1 minute, and then move to a wire rack to cool completely.

TO MAKE THE FROSTING:

Beat the butter with an electric mixer on medium speed until light and fluffy, about 1 to 2 minutes. Slowly add the powdered sugar, vanilla bean, vanilla extract, and salt while continuously beating.

Add the heavy cream, starting with just 1 tablespoon, and add more if needed to make the perfect frosting consistency.

Frost the cupcakes with the vanilla bean frosting and serve.

PERFECT HOMEMADE SPRINKLES CUPCAKES

The happiest batch of cupcakes you've ever seen. You'll smile the whole time you bake them, and you'll smile the most as you eat them. *Makes 6 cupcakes*

FOR THE CUPCAKES:

4 tablespoons unsalted butter, melted

⅓ cup + 1 tablespoon granulated sugar

1 large egg white

1 teaspoon vanilla

⅔ cup all-purpose flour

¾ teaspoon baking powder

⅛ teaspoon baking soda

⅛ teaspoon fine sea salt

3 tablespoons whole milk

2 tablespoons colorful sprinkles

FOR THE FROSTING:

4 tablespoons unsalted butter, at room temperature

½ cup powdered sugar

1 tablespoon milk

1 tablespoon sprinkles

Preheat the oven to 350°F and line a muffin pan with six liners.

Melt the butter and stir in the sugar very well.

Next, stir in the egg white and vanilla. Stir until very well mixed.

Sprinkle the flour, baking powder, baking soda, and salt evenly over the mixture.

Stir to combine while slowly adding the milk.

Finally, stir in the sprinkles.

Divide the batter among the cupcake liners and bake for 15 to 17 minutes, until the tops of the cupcakes are set and spring back when lightly touched.

Let the cupcakes cool completely, leaving them in the muffin pan.

While the cupcakes are cooling, make the frosting: Beat together the butter and powdered sugar. Only add the milk if the frosting needs help coming together into a light, fluffy mixture. Stir in the sprinkles right before frosting the cupcakes and serving them.

MARSHMALLOW-FILLED CUPCAKES

This recipe for homemade Ding-Dongs is really just another way to use my One-Bowl Chocolate Cupcakes (on page 80). The cupcakes bake up perfectly flat, so it's easy to stuff with fluff and dip the top in melted chocolate. You just might want to double this recipe . . . *Makes 4 individual cakes*

1 recipe chocolate cupcakes (see page 80)

¼ cup marshmallow fluff (any flavor)

2 tablespoons unsalted butter, softened

⅓ cup chopped chocolate (milk, bittersweet, whatever you like)

1 teaspoon coconut oil

Prepare the chocolate cupcakes from page 80.

In a small bowl, beat together the marshmallow fluff and butter until light and fluffy.

Scrape the marshmallow mixture into a piping bag (or plastic bag with the tip cut off) and insert a large frosting tip.

Pipe the marshmallow filling into the center of each cupcake. (See photo for reference.)

Watch the surface of the cupcakes carefully as you pipe the marshmallow filling inside—they will slightly puff up when they're full.

Next, melt the chocolate and coconut oil in 30-second increments in the microwave at full power. Dunk each cupcake upside down in the melted chocolate and let set before serving.

PEPPERMINT BROWNIE BITES

I can always seem to find a reason to bake four little brownie bites. No matter the season, these brownie bites are welcome. When peppermint doesn't sound good, sprinkles do. Or mini chocolate chips. Or crushed cookies. You have seriously delicious options with this recipe! *Makes 4 mini brownies*

FOR THE BROWNIE BITES:

3 tablespoons unsalted butter, plus extra for greasing the pan

7 tablespoons granulated sugar

¼ cup cocoa powder

¼ teaspoon fine sea salt

¼ teaspoon peppermint extract

1 large egg

3 tablespoons all-purpose flour

FOR DUNKING:

½ cup chopped chocolate

1 tablespoon coconut oil

10 peppermint candies, crushed

Preheat the oven to 350°F and grease four cups in a muffin pan very well with butter.

Next, combine the butter, sugar, and cocoa powder in a small bowl and microwave at full power for 30 seconds. Stir very well and repeat.

Stir the salt and vanilla into the warm batter, then stir for about a minute to cool off the mixture. Then stir in the egg.

Finally, sprinkle the flour over the top and stir into the batter using about 50 strokes. (You want to stir the flour very well to activate the gluten and make a chewy brownie.)

Bake the bites for 15 minutes, then remove from the oven.

Fill a shallow bowl with crushed peppermint candies for dipping.

Meanwhile, add the chopped chocolate and coconut oil to a small bowl. Microwave at 50 percent power for 30 seconds. Stir and repeat. After 1 minute, a few unmelted pieces of chocolate may remain, but that's fine: Let the mixture rest on the counter for 1 minute and stir again. It should all be smooth by now.

Take each warm brownie bite from the pan, dunk in chocolate, and roll in crushed peppermint.

I usually serve these warm, but if you want the chocolate to harden, place them in the fridge for 15 minutes.

Arguably the cutest thing you can do with a muffin pan. While these look intricate and complicated, using store-bought refrigerated crust and a pizza dough cutter will set you on your way in no time.

I use raspberries because, with a little almond extract, they make my favorite pie, but any berries you love will work here. Blueberries and orange zest? Concord grapes and vanilla? Go for it! *Makes 4 mini pies*

MINI RASPBERRY PIES

1 sheet refrigerated, premade pie crust

Butter (for greasing the pan)

10 ounces fresh raspberries

3 tablespoons granulated sugar

3 tablespoons all-purpose flour

½ teaspoon almond extract

1 teaspoon lemon juice

1 egg yolk, beaten (for glaze)

Coarse sugar (optional)

Remove the dough from the fridge about 15 minutes before you want to bake.

Preheat the oven to 350°F and butter four cups in a muffin pan VERY WELL.

Lightly roll out the dough to make it about ½-inch larger in diameter than it is. You will be cutting out four 5-inch circles and using the scraps for the lattice work.

Cut out 5-inch circles using a glass or a biscuit cutter.

Press a circle of dough into each cup. The circles should come up to the top of the cups, maybe slightly higher.

Gather up the pie dough scraps and roll flat again. Use a pizza wheel to cut 7 tiny strips of dough for each pie (that's 28 strips of dough, each about 4 inches long). Flour them well, pile them on a plate, and place the plate in the fridge while you make the filling.

Combine the fresh raspberries, flour, sugar, almond extract, and lemon juice in a bowl. Stir very well. The raspberries will start to break down.

Divide the raspberry mixture between each cup.

Remove the lattice strips from the fridge and lay four across each mini pie. Carefully (and quickly!), loosely weave in three other strips in the opposite direction. It's not a perfect lattice, but it'll be just fine!

Brush each pie with egg yolk and sprinkle with coarse sugar.

Bake the pies for about 20 minutes, until golden brown and the filling is bubbling.

Let the pies cool for 15 minutes, then run a knife around the edges to loosen them.

Remove the pies from the pan to cool completely on a wire rack (don't let them cool in the pan, as they might stick terribly).

CHOCOLATE FRUIT BARK

I'm trying to be better about keeping homemade snacks on hand. A few bites of this chocolate bark with fresh fruit on top will hold me over until dinner.

I make this chocolate bark in a muffin pan with muffin liners to help keep my portion control in check. Feel free to substitute whatever kind of fresh fruit you want to use here. And if you're out of muffin liners, just spread it on a mini baking sheet, chill, and break into pieces. *Makes 8 candies*

⅓ cup pomegranate arils

¼ cup coconut flakes

1 cup chocolate chips

1 tablespoon coconut oil

Line a muffin pan with eight paper liners.

Place the pomegranate arils and coconut flakes in two small bowls nearby.

Place the chocolate chips and coconut oil in a medium-size microwave-safe bowl.

Turn the microwave to 50 percent power and heat the chocolate chips in 15-second increments, stopping between each increment to stir. You should remove the chocolate from the microwave before it melts fully—about 3 to 4 increments should do the trick.

Let the chocolate sit on the counter in the warm bowl, stirring occasionally until it melts fully.

Using a tablespoon, scoop the melted chocolate into the paper liners.

Immediately after scooping the chocolate, sprinkle the pomegranate and coconut on top.

Chill the fruit bark in the fridge for about 15 minutes to harden. Store in the fridge.

Deep, dark, rich chocolate pound cakes are the best thing to go with a cup of something hot for breakfast. You have the rest of the day to make better nutrition choices. *Makes 4 individual cakes*

MINI CHOCOLATE POUND CAKES
with Raspberry Sauce

FOR THE CAKES:

⅓ cup (2 ounces) semisweet chocolate chips

3 tablespoons unsalted butter, softened

3 tablespoons granulated sugar

1 large egg

½ teaspoon vanilla extract

6 tablespoons all-purpose flour

2 tablespoons unsweetened cocoa powder

¼ teaspoon baking powder

Pinch of fine sea salt

1 tablespoon warm water

FRESH RASPBERRY SAUCE:

1 (6-ounce) container fresh raspberries

2 teaspoons lemon juice

1 tablespoon honey

EASY TIP: *If you make the pound cakes ahead of time, rewarm them in the microwave for 8 seconds to soften them before serving.*

TO MAKE THE CAKES:

First, preheat the oven to 350°F and line four cups in a muffin pan with cupcake liners.

Next, in a small microwave-safe bowl, melt the chocolate chips. To do this, heat them in the microwave at 50 percent power in 20-second intervals. Stir between each interval. Remove from the microwave before everything is completely melted and stir to combine until the chocolate is smooth and silky.

In a separate medium-size bowl, beat the butter and sugar together with an electric mixer on medium speed until light and fluffy, 1 minute. Next, beat in the egg and vanilla extract.

Stream the melted chocolate into the butter-sugar mixture and beat until combined.

Next, combine the flour, cocoa powder, baking powder, and pinch of salt in a small bowl. Whisk it all together with a fork.

Add half of the dry ingredients to the wet ingredients, stirring just to combine. Add the warm water and stir to combine. Finally, add the last of the dry ingredients and stir until no lumps remain, but do not overmix.

Divide the batter between the four cupcake liners and bake for 18 to 20 minutes. When done, the top will appear dry and spring back when touched.

Serve immediately with raspberry sauce (recipe below).

TO MAKE THE RASPBERRY SAUCE:

Combine all ingredients in a small saucepan. Bring to a boil and cook until the raspberries dissolve, about 3 minutes. Strain the mixture and serve with the chocolate pound cakes.

As I've somewhat shamefully admitted before, I try to withhold sugar from my daughter, Camille. I just feel like growing up as the daughter of a baker will lead to an excess of sugar in her life. I'm trying to delay the inevitable.

When it came time to celebrate Camille's first birthday (a truly glorious day, as my postpartum depression had finally lifted just a week prior), I had visions of going all out with a cake with gobs of frosting and sprinkles for her to smear everywhere. I envisioned the perfect photograph I'd capture as she tasted her first bite of white sugar.

In the end, I couldn't do it. She is such a good little eater—she loves broccoli, plain yogurt, and sauerkraut—I was afraid to ruin her palate.

I compromised and developed a recipe for maple syrup cupcakes with coconut whipped cream frosting.

In the end, it turns out that no matter what kind of cake you give a kid, if you stick a hat on them with an elastic strap around their chin, they are going to scream. *Makes 8 cupcakes*

CAMILLE'S CUPCAKES
Maple Syrup Cupcakes + Coconut Whip

FOR THE CUPCAKES:

3 tablespoons
unsalted butter, melted

1 tablespoon neutral oil

⅔ cup maple syrup

1 large egg

1 cup all-purpose flour

1 teaspoon baking powder

¼ teaspoon fine sea salt

½ cup whole milk

**FOR THE COCONUT
WHIPPED CREAM:**

1 can (14-ounces) of coconut cream,
refrigerated overnight (see note)

1½ tablespoons maple syrup

EASY TIP: *You really should refrigerate the can AND the bowl you want to beat the whipped cream in overnight. It makes the cream whip up more quickly.*

Preheat the oven to 325°F and line eight cups in a muffin pan with cupcake liners.

In a medium-size bowl, beat the melted butter and oil with an electric mixer.

Stream in the maple syrup and keep beating.

Next, add the egg and beat until combined.

Sprinkle the flour, baking powder, and salt evenly over the batter, and beat for a few seconds just to combine, then add all of the milk at once.

Beat everything until smooth, scraping down the sides of the bowl as you go.

Divide the mixture into the prepared cups and bake for 20 minutes.

When the cupcakes are totally cool, make the coconut whipped cream: scrape all of the coconut cream out of the can and into a cold bowl (do not add the little bit of coconut water or juice in the can—just the thick, white cream).

Beat with an electric mixer on HIGH until light and fluffy, about 2 to 3 minutes. Add the maple syrup and beat to combine.

Taste the frosting—if you want it sweeter, you're going to have to add powdered sugar because any more maple syrup will make it too thin to pipe.

Frost the cupcakes and serve.

OLIVE OIL CAKELETS

If you've never made a cake with fruity olive oil, I have to say you're really missing out. I've always found that oil makes cakes more tender (because butter is solid at room temperature while oil is not). You need to reach for a high-quality, fruity olive oil that you would use for salad dressing. I love Arbequina olive oil from California.

I amp up the flavor even more with citrus zest, juice, and toasted almonds. Use your favorite citrus (I like Meyer lemon and bergamot!) and your favorite nuts.

I happen to know that Camille loves to find half of one of these cakelets in her lunch box. *Makes 6 individual cakes*

½ cup + 3 tablespoons all-purpose flour

½ cup granulated sugar, plus extra for topping

½ teaspoon fine sea salt

¼ teaspoon baking powder

⅛ teaspoon baking soda

6 tablespoons fruity extra virgin olive oil

6 tablespoons whole milk

1 large egg

½ teaspoon fresh citrus zest

2 tablespoons fresh citrus juice

¼ teaspoon almond extract

¼ cup sliced almonds for topping

Preheat the oven to 350°F and line six cups in a muffin pan with paper liners (or use pretty freestanding cupcake liners like I did here).

In a small bowl, whisk together the flour, sugar, salt, baking powder, and baking soda.

In a measuring cup, whisk together the oil, milk, egg, citrus zest and juice, and almond extract.

Add the wet ingredients to the dry and stir just until combined.

Divide the batter among the cups, then sprinkle the almonds on top. Add a pinch of sugar on top of the almonds before sliding the pan into the oven.

Bake for 30 minutes, then test with a toothpick—moist crumbs should cling to it, but no wet batter should remain.

I like these best served warm, right from the oven.

RAMEKINS
&
SMALL JARS

CHERRY COBBLER

For this recipe, I used classic 4-ounce ramekins, but I used the ones that are wider than they are deep (about 5 inches wide instead of 3½). I did this because I'm obsessed with the little heart-shaped dough pieces that go on top and I wanted to show them off more, but a regular ramekin will still work. You won't need as many hearts for a smaller ramekin, though.

Because the best cherries for pies and cobblers are tart cherries, and because I've never lived in a state where I can find them fresh, I'm calling for frozen ones here. They can still be tricky to find in the South, though, so if you end up using regular sweet cherries like I have to sometimes, reduce the sugar to ½ teaspoon.

My heart-shaped cutter is only ½-inch wide and is specifically made for cutting vents in pie crust. You can use any other shape you like—but let's all agree that mini hearts are the cutest! *Fills two 4-ounce ramekins*

1 refrigerated piecrust

1½ cups frozen tart cherries

2 tablespoons granulated sugar

1 teaspoon lemon juice

½ teaspoon almond extract

1 teaspoon cornstarch

1 egg yolk, beaten

Coarse sugar, for sprinkling

Preheat the oven to 400°F.

Let the pie crust rest at room temperature for about 10 minutes to soften. Unroll it and use a heart-shaped cookie cutter to cut out about 50 to 60 little dough hearts. Lightly sprinkle the hearts with flour while tossing gently, then set aside.

Combine the cherries, sugar, lemon juice, almond extract, and cornstarch in a bowl. Toss very well to combine.

Divide the cherry mixture among the ramekins.

Place the dough hearts on top of the cherry mixture in each ramekin. I like to pile them all to one side, making two layers, and then put a few stray ones on the bare side for effect.

Brush beat egg yolk on top of the dough hearts. Sprinkle coarse sugar on top.

Bake for 20 to 25 minutes, until the dough hearts are golden brown and the cherries are bubbling.

LITTLE BROWNIE POTS

So little, but so big on flavor. These look unassuming, but let me fill you in: You're about to experience a warm, gooey brownie with a molten chocolate center, topped with ice cream. The two melt and mingle and make the world just right. *Fills two 4-ounce ramekins*

4 tablespoons unsalted butter

½ cup granulated sugar

¼ cup + 2 tablespoons cocoa powder

¼ teaspoon fine sea salt

½ teaspoon vanilla extract

1 large egg

¼ cup all-purpose flour

2 scoops of your favorite ice cream

Preheat the oven to 350°F and place the ramekins on a small baking sheet.

In a medium-size microwave-safe bowl, heat the butter, sugar, and cocoa powder at full power for 30 seconds. Stop, stir, and return to the microwave for another 30 seconds. The butter should be completely melted, and as you stir, the mixture should become fully blended and smooth.

Let the mixture cool for 1 minute.

Stir in the salt and vanilla.

Finally, stir in the egg.

Next, add the flour and stir for about 50 brisk strokes. You're activating the gluten in the flour to make a chewy brownie.

Divide the batter between the two ramekins.

Bake on a baking sheet for 19 to 20 minutes. When done, the brownies will be dry on the top and molten in the center—YUM!

Place the ramekins on a serving plate, top with ice cream, and serve.

EGGNOG BREAD PUDDING

My friend Phi Kelnhofer (she blogs at sweetphi.com) decoded the mystery of making individual portions of bread pudding in ramekins. I'm just here to spread her gospel.

I used eggnog as a fun seasonal twist on her recipe. I also topped it with way too much nutmeg, but that's just the way I like it.

Fills two 4-ounce ramekins

2 large eggs

6 tablespoons store-bought eggnog

2 tablespoons granulated sugar, plus extra for sprinkling

1 teaspoon whiskey

¼ teaspoon freshly grated nutmeg, plus extra for serving

2 slices fresh white bread, diced

Freshly whipped cream, for serving

Preheat the oven to 350°F and line a small baking sheet with foil. (If the mixture spills over in the oven, it will pretty much ruin your pan. Use foil!)

Spray the ramekins with cooking spray.

In a medium-size bowl, whisk together the eggs, eggnog, 2 tablespoons of the sugar, the whiskey, and the nutmeg.

Add the bread cubes and stir to coat.

Equally divide the mixture between the two ramekins and sprinkle a big pinch of sugar over each one.

Bake for 32 to 35 minutes, until puffed and lightly golden brown.

Serve warm with whipped cream and freshly grated nutmeg.

NO-BAKE CHEESECAKES

There's a restaurant in downtown Davis, California, with cheesecake on the dessert menu. Okay, okay, I know that describes almost every restaurant, but Bistro 33 is different—the cheesecake comes to the table unapologetically, in a ramekin without a crust. And while normal cheesecake fans would complain about this, they are silenced at the first bite. There's something so great and simple about a few bites of cheesecake in a ramekin that you don't have to share. Not every cheesecake needs to be complicated and towering high on the plate.

If you glance through the ingredient list, you'll see that this recipe is easily doubled or tripled to serve a crowd.

Some people call this my "cheesecake mousse" recipe because the cheesecake is so light and fluffy. I call it "addicting." *Fills two 4-ounce ramekins*

4 ounces cream cheese, at room temperature

¼ cup heavy whipping cream

½ cup powdered sugar

½ teaspoon vanilla extract

Fresh berries, for serving

In a small bowl, beat the cream cheese with an electric mixer on HIGH until it's soft and creamy, about 30 seconds.

In another small bowl, beat the whipping cream until soft peaks form. Beat in the powdered sugar and vanilla.

Add half of the whipped cream to the cream cheese and beat on medium speed until combined. Repeat with the remaining half.

Divide the cheesecake between the two ramekins.

Cover and refrigerate for at least 4 hours.

Serve with fresh berries.

CHEESECAKE DIP FOR TWO

When I meet strangers in public and they ask what I do for a living, somehow this cheesecake dip always comes up. I explain to them I'm all about small desserts that are easy to make, and if they give me a confused face, I say, "You know how hard it is to make a big cheesecake? I took those flavors and made it into an easy dip." And suddenly they get my concept and a fierce cheesecake craving hits.

I'm considering printing this recipe on the back of my business cards.

Makes about 1 cup

4 ounces cream cheese, softened

¼ cup plain Greek yogurt

½ teaspoon vanilla extract

1 tablespoon unsalted butter

2 tablespoons dark brown sugar

The rest of the can of pie cherries from the recipe for Cheesecake in a Loaf Pan (see page 51)

In a small bowl, beat together the cream cheese, Greek yogurt, and vanilla with an electric mixer on high speed. Beat very well, until it's smooth and creamy. You really can't overbeat this mixture. Fluffy is what we're going after.

Next, melt the butter and brown sugar together, either in a small bowl in the microwave or in a small pan on the stove. Let the butter gently sizzle and stir until the brown sugar dissolves fully.

Beat the butter-brown sugar mixture (a.k.a. HEAVEN) into the cream cheese mixture.

Plate the cheesecake mixture and top with canned pie cherries (or any other fruit you like!).

CANNOLI DIP

When I think of the great city of Philadelphia, my mind jumps to Reading Terminal Market. You can't go wrong with any type of sandwich in that building. You are also required to leave the building with a cannoli in hand. Ahhhh, the cannoli stop—where the bags of sweet ricotta filling are packed tight and hung from the ceiling for easy filling. The crisp cannoli shells somehow manage to be easy to bite through, yet don't shatter completely. It's magic. And it's also magic how much this dip will cure your Philly cannoli craving in a fraction of the time! *Makes 1 cup*

1 cup whole milk ricotta cheese

¼ cup powdered sugar

2 tablespoons heavy cream (or milk)

¼ teaspoon vanilla extract

¼ teaspoon almond extract

Mini chocolate chips, for serving

3 to 4 large waffle cones, broken into pieces

In a food processor, combine the ricotta, powdered sugar, cream, vanilla, and almond extract. Purée until light and fluffy, about 15 seconds.

Scrape the mixture into a serving bowl and top with extra powdered sugar and mini chocolate chips. Serve with waffle cone chips.

SLOW COOKER CRÈME BRÛLÉE

My love of crème brûlée runs deep. It has to do with an egg custard aversion that started early in life—I am very much making up for lost time.

I would absolutely hate it if you never ate homemade crème brûlée because you were scared of getting the bake just right.

Enter your slow cooker. Just one hour on low in your slow cooker, and you're guaranteed to have perfect custard! Now go—pick up one of those kitchen torches you've always wanted. *Fills two 4-ounce ramekins*

3 large egg yolks

½ cup heavy whipping cream

¼ cup + 2 teaspoons granulated sugar

¼ of a vanilla bean
(or 1 teaspoon vanilla extract)

Combine the egg yolks, whipping cream, and ¼ cup of the sugar in a bowl. Whisk to combine.

Using a dull knife, scrape the seeds out of the vanilla bean and add it to the cream mixture. (You should have about ⅛ teaspoon of vanilla bean seeds.)

Whisk the mixture together very well.

Meanwhile, take two 12-inch-long pieces of foil and roll them up into "snake" shapes. Then curl each one into a circle and pinch the ends together. Place them side by side in the bottom of your slow cooker.

Place each ramekin on top of each foil ring.

Carefully pour boiling water into the slow cooker (don't splash water on the custards!) until the water reaches about one-third of the way up the side of the ramekins.

Turn the slow cooker to LOW and cook for 2 to 2½ hours. When done, the custards should be set—poke one with a knife to be sure.

Cover and chill the custards at least 6 hours.

Before serving, sprinkle the remaining 2 teaspoons of sugar evenly over both custards and torch with a culinary torch until brown.

EARL GREY CRÈME BRÛLÉE

Truth be told, I made this crème brûlée accidentally one day. I had a little splash of heavy cream that was about to expire, and I wanted to put it to good use. That's one of the many things I love about small-batch desserts: a small amount of a few ingredients can make something completely fabulous.

Anyway, I wanted a spin on my traditional crème brûlée, and I happened to be sipping a warm cup of Earl Grey tea at the same time. And I had an idea.

I steeped two tea bags in the cream and went about making my crème brûlée as usual. (You can definitely do this in the slow cooker, using the method from page 120.) As expected, the final result was a dream come true.

Feel free to use your favorite type of tea, or even substitute 1 tablespoon of instant coffee. (See, I didn't forget about you coffee lovers out there!)

Fills two 4-ounce ramekins

½ cup heavy whipping cream

1 or 2 bags of your favorite tea (use 1 for a light flavor, 2 for a very strong flavor)

3 egg yolks

¼ cup + 2 teaspoons granulated sugar

In a small saucepan, add the cream and tea bag(s). Turn the heat to medium-low and bring to a gentle simmer. Turn off the heat, cover, and let steep for 20 minutes.

Strain the mixture into a bowl.

Whisk in the egg yolks and ¼ cup of sugar.

Pour into the ramekins. Place the ramekins in an 8- or 9-inch square glass baking dish. Make a water bath for them to cook in by pouring 2 cups of very hot water into the dish, or enough to come about ½ inch up on the sides of the ramekins.

Bake at 300°F for 45 to 50 minutes. The custards are done when only the middle is slightly jiggly.

Cool the custards in the water bath, then cover them with plastic wrap before moving them to the fridge for at least 8 hours.

When ready to caramelize the sugar with a kitchen torch, sprinkle 1 teaspoon of sugar over each custard. Melt the sugar with the torch until it is browned and crispy. Serve immediately.

GINGERBREAD FLAN

I can hardly get enough gingerbread in my life when the weather is cool. I love a good gingerbread cake (try my version with the Lemon Glaze on page 165), and a warm gingerbread latte is a pretty stellar way to start the day too. I wanted to work gingerbread into a make-ahead date night dessert, and this gingerbread flan was born. *Fills two 4-ounce ramekins*

3 tablespoons granulated sugar

1 large egg + 1 large egg yolk

½ cup half-and-half

2 tablespoons molasses

¼ teaspoon ground ginger

¼ teaspoon ground cinnamon

Dash of ground cloves

Dash of freshly grated nutmeg

¼ teaspoon vanilla extract

Preheat the oven to 325°F. Have ready two 4-ounce ramekins and one 8-inch square baking dish, preferably made of ceramic or a heavy material (not metal).

Measure the granulated sugar into a small saucepan. Cover the pot and turn the heat to medium-high. After 2 minutes, remove the lid and tilt the sugar gently to help it melt. Set the pan back on the heat and monitor it until all the sugar melts and turns an amber color. Keep a close eye on it—it goes from caramel to burnt very quickly. This process should take 5 to 7 minutes.

Once the caramel is amber colored, immediately pour it into the two awaiting ramekins. It will harden right away.

Next, whisk together the whole egg, egg yolk, half-and-half, molasses, spices, and vanilla extract. Whisk it well, but be careful—you don't want to create too many bubbles. The custard should be smooth. (Let the custard set for a few minutes if too many bubbles appear.)

Next, strain the mixture into a glass measuring cup with a pour spout. Gently pop any bubbles on the surface, or let it sit for a few minutes until most of the bubbles pop.

Pour the custard mixture over the caramel in the ramekins.

Set the ramekins in the baking dish.

Carefully pour 2 to 3 cups of hot water into the baking dish. The water should come halfway up the sides of the ramekins.

Bake the custards for 33 to 36 minutes. The edges will set and the middles will be ever-so-slightly jiggly. Jiggly like Jell-O, not like milk.

Let the ramekins cool in the water bath for 10 minutes, then wrap them in plastic wrap and refrigerate overnight. You don't want to rush this step. The longer the custards sit, the softer the caramel will get so it easily pours over the plate when unmolded.

When ready to serve, run a thin knife around the edge of the ramekins. To release a flan, quickly turn the ramekin upside down on the plate. Let it sit for a few minutes. If caramel doesn't begin to run out, gently use a knife to coax the custard from its dish.

Serve chilled.

EASY BAKED ALASKA (no, really!)

So what is Baked Alaska and why do you need it in your life? (I'm so glad I'm here to answer these important life questions for you!)

Baked Alaska is an old-fashioned dessert. It is a slice of pound cake with a scoop of ice cream or sorbet on top and a torched meringue (think: marshmallow) coating. Yes, there are fancier versions of it—with multiple layers of ice cream and sorbets and such—but this is the simple version.

So, we're going to buy a premade pound cake at the store. Check the bakery section or even the freezer for the one that looks the best. Grab a chocolate or lemon one, whatever you like the most! The day I photographed this recipe for you, I grabbed vanilla.

Next, grab your favorite ice cream or sorbet. I always reach for raspberry.

And then grab your stash of leftover egg whites from making all the earlier small-batch cookie recipes. Do you have a kitchen torch for making crème brûlée? If so, you're going to use it again here. If not, I recommend you make the investment now!

I'll write the recipe as if you're making it for two, but obviously the number of servings you make depends on how many slices of pound cake and how many pints of ice cream you bought. Scale it up, scale it down, whatever you need to do. If you're just making it for two, I have a fun way to use up the rest of the pound cake on the next page. *Makes 2 servings*

2 slices premade
vanilla pound cake

2 scoops raspberry sorbet,
slightly softened

2 large egg whites

3 tablespoons
granulated sugar

First, cut two 1-inch-thick slices of pound cake. Using a 4-ounce ramekin as the size guide, cut out a circle from each slice to fit on top of the ramekins perfectly. Set the cake circles aside on separate plates.

Next, line two ramekins with plastic wrap. Scoop the sorbet and press it into a ramekin. You can press it totally flat or make it domed on top for the classic look.

Place the ramekins back in the freezer and chill until very firm.

Once the sorbet is firm, use the plastic wrap to lift out each scoop of sorbet. Remove the wrap and place the sorbet on top of each pound cake circle. Press it firmly to help it adhere to the cake, cover in plastic wrap, and return to the freezer for at least 1 hour. (You can do this up to a day in advance if you cover it with plastic wrap.)

Right before serving, make the meringue: Add the egg whites and sugar to a medium-size bowl. Beat on high with an electric mixer until soft, shiny peaks form. Don't overbeat—soft peaks are the goal.

Remove the cakes from the freezer. Using a small offset spatula, spread half of the egg white mixture on top of each cake. (For fun, drag a fork through the meringue to make a fun design once torched.)

Hold a kitchen torch about 4 inches away from the cakes and lightly toast the meringue with the flame on high. It will almost immediately turn golden brown—YUM!

Stand back and admire your work—it's very impressive!

Serve immediately.

Note: If you don't have a blowtorch, spread the egg whites onto the sorbet, then freeze for 2 hours. Heat the broiler and place the desserts on a rimmed baking sheet a few inches from the broiler until browned evenly. Watch them closely and rotate as needed. Serve immediately.

EASIEST POUND CAKE LAYER CAKES

Okay, okay, you're finally catching on about how lazy I can be about baking. I had leftover pound cake from making the Baked Alaskas (page 127), and I used a ramekin to cut out circles, stacked them with whipped cream, and served them as individual layer cakes. And guess what? No one complained about it at all!

And now, get ready, because we're going to use that leftover pound cake.

Makes 2 individual cakes

6 slices leftover pound cake

¾ cup heavy whipping cream

1 orange, zested

1 teaspoon orange liqueur (optional)

½ cup powdered sugar

Fresh strawberries, for serving

Place a bowl in the freezer for about 30 minutes to chill.

Use a 4-ounce ramekin to trace circles to cut out of each slice of pound cake (or use a round cookie cutter).

Pour the heavy cream in the chilled bowl and beat until soft peaks form. Add the powdered sugar, orange zest, and orange liqueur (if using). Beat until firm peaks form.

Place one pound cake circle on each of two serving plates.

Top with a layer of whipped cream.

Stack and repeat until you have three layers of cake and whipped cream.

Top the final cakes with sliced fresh strawberries and serve.

SKINNY CHEESECAKE WITH STRAWBERRIES

I feel like we have quite a few variations of cheesecake in this book. It's such an easy, simple (and make-ahead!) dessert. I knew I had to include this lighter version made with yogurt. I don't feel one bit guilty eating it for breakfast.

You can use regular ramekins or small glass jars for this dessert.

Makes 2 servings

FOR THE CHEESECAKES:

1 cup 2% plain Greek yogurt

⅓ cup granulated sugar

1 large egg

½ teaspoon vanilla bean paste (or 1 teaspoon extract)

1½ teaspoons cornstarch

FOR THE TOPPING:

2 cups strawberries, cored and sliced

Drizzle of honey

Extra yogurt, for garnish

Preheat the oven to 375°F and fit two mini 1-cup jars into a baking dish. Fill the baking dish with water so the water comes up the sides of the jars about 1 inch. Set aside.

In a mini food processor, combine the yogurt, sugar, egg, vanilla, and cornstarch. Pulse until well blended.

Divide the mixture between the jars and bake for 23 to 26 minutes—the tops will appear set and may even start to turn very light brown.

Cover the jars and chill in the fridge for at least 4 hours.

Meanwhile, make the strawberry topping: in a small saucepan, combine the sliced strawberries with a splash of water.

Cook over medium heat until they collapse and the sauce starts to thicken, about 5 minutes.

Remove from heat and stir in honey to taste.

Let the strawberry sauce cool, then divide it evenly on top of the cheesecake jars.

Garnish with extra yogurt and more fresh strawberries.

CHAI PUDDING
+ Gingersnap Crumbles

It's a bit hard for me to put words to my feelings for this recipe. Warm, spicy chai pudding—I couldn't dream up anything better to eat! I googled it, and it's never been done before. And it's so delicious I can hardly believe it.

While this pudding is great served chilled like regular pudding, it really shines when served warm, especially over a slice of chocolate cake.

Makes 2 servings

½ cup granulated sugar

2 tablespoons cornstarch

⅛ teaspoon fine sea salt

1¼ cup milk

½ cup heavy cream

1 large egg yolk

½ teaspoon cinnamon

¼ teaspoon cardamom

¼ teaspoon ground cloves (or 1 whole clove in the milk mixture)

¼ teaspoon allspice

2 slices of fresh ginger, 1-inch thick, smashed

1 tablespoon unsalted butter

½ teaspoon vanilla

8 gingersnap cookies, crushed, for serving

In a medium-size glass bowl, combine the sugar, cornstarch, salt, and spices. Stir with a whisk to blend very well. (If you're using a whole clove instead of ground cloves, add it to the milk to steep while cooking and then remove before serving.)

Slowly pour in ¼ cup of the cream and whisk vigorously to dissolve the sugar and cornstarch. Add the last of the cream slowly, still whisking.

Add the milk slowly and whisk very well to ensure all the dry ingredients are dissolved.

Pour the milk and cream mixture into a saucepan and add the smashed ginger slices.

Put the saucepan on the stove over medium heat. Bring the pudding to a simmer while constantly stirring with a wooden spoon. Be sure to scrape the sides and bottom of the saucepan during cooking.

Place the egg yolk in a separate small bowl and have it ready on the side.

When the pudding starts to gently simmer, turn the heat to low. Ladle a small amount (about 2 tablespoons) of the pudding into the bowl with the egg yolk and whisk very well. Repeat three times. Pour the egg yolk and pudding mixture back into the pan with the rest of the pudding.

Bring the pudding back to a gentle simmer and cook another one minute. Turn off the heat and stir in the butter and vanilla.

Remove the ginger slices (and whole clove, if used).

Pour the pudding into two small cups, cover with plastic wrap, and refrigerate at least 4 hours before serving. (If you don't like pudding skin, press the plastic wrap directly on the surface of the pudding before chilling.)

Before serving, remove the plastic wrap and top with the crushed gingersnap cookies.

SECRET INGREDIENT CHOCOLATE MOUSSE

I almost didn't want to tell you there is avocado in this mousse. You won't even notice it. Seriously!

I don't include avocado for the health benefits (though there are some great ones) or because my daughter and I share an avocado almost every day. I use avocado in my mousse because it makes mousse come together in a fraction of the time—way less work and way less chilling time!

If you've ever tried to make "real" chocolate mousse, it can be finicky. The eggs must be just the right temperature and the folding technique must be spot-on. You won't find any of those difficult directions in this recipe. Basically, you dump everything into the food processor and blend.

When I call for coconut cream, I'm referring to the cream from the top of a can of full-fat coconut milk. It's super thick and resembles whipped cream when chilled. They now sell entire cans of just coconut cream at some stores, but if you can't find it, just skim the top off a can of regular (not light) coconut milk. *Makes 2 servings*

½ cup semisweet chocolate chips

2 small, very ripe avocados (no brown spots, though!)

¼ cup unsweetened cocoa powder

¼ cup maple syrup

2 to 3 tablespoons coconut cream (from the can)

2 teaspoons vanilla extract

⅛ teaspoon fine fine sea salt

A handful of raspberries, for serving

In a small microwave-safe bowl, add the chocolate chips. Microwave at 50 percent power in 30-second increments, until melted entirely. Stir between each increment.

In the bowl of a food processor, add all ingredients except the raspberries (including the melted chocolate). Start with 2 tablespoons of coconut cream, and you can add more after blending if you need it.

Purée for at least 1 minute—avocado chunks in this mousse are the devil.

Taste the mousse—add more maple syrup if you need it. Add more coconut cream if it seems a bit too thick.

To serve, drop three or four raspberries into the bottom of each serving cup.

Top with ¼ of the mousse in each cup.

Add another layer of raspberries before dividing the last of the mousse between both cups.

Cover and chill the mousse for a few hours.

Sprinkle a few more raspberries on top before serving.

EASY TIP: *You can serve the mousse right out of the food processor, but it does firm up nicely (and taste slightly better) chilled.*

BERRY-MISU

Often, I get asked what my favorite dessert is. I usually answer with "pavlova." That is, until I made this citrus-kissed berry tiramisu. I could eat this dessert anytime and never grow tired of it. It's best, of course, when all the summer berries are fresh, but I've been known to make it with a bag of frozen mixed berries too. In that case, I defrost the berries, drain off the juice, and replace it with even more Chambord.

If you haven't stumbled across Chambord, or raspberry liqueur, it's worth seeking out. I love a splash in hot chocolate in the winter. Suitable replacements are crème de cassis (blackcurrant liqueur) or Cointreau (orange liqueur). *Makes 2 to 4 servings*

3 cups mixed fresh berries (strawberries, blackberries, blueberries, and raspberries), washed

2 tablespoons Chambord (raspberry liqueur)

4 tablespoons powdered sugar, divided

8 ounces mascarpone cheese, softened

1 medium navel orange

Half a 3-ounce package of store-bought soft ladyfingers

Slice the strawberries into bite-size pieces and combine in a bowl with the other berries. Sprinkle the Chambord on the berries and stir to combine.

Stir in 2 tablespoons of the powdered sugar and let rest for 10 minutes. As the berries sit, they will start to release their juices.

Meanwhile, in a small bowl, stir together the softened mascarpone and the other 2 tablespoons of powdered sugar.

Zest the orange into the mascarpone mixture.

Juice the orange and add it to the mascarpone. Stir very well and set aside.

Place four 4-ounce ramekins (or two larger serving bowls) in front of you.

Place a small scoop of fresh berries on the bottom of each ramekin or bowl.

Place one or two ladyfingers on top of the berries.

Spread a thin layer of the mascarpone mixture on top of the ladyfingers.

Repeat the process: berries, ladyfingers, mascarpone, twice in each dish, ending with the remaining berries on top.

Cover the dishes with plastic wrap and refrigerate for at least 4 hours to let the dessert soften and meld together.

Remove the plastic wrap from the berry-misu about 15 minutes before you plan to serve it to allow the mascarpone mixture to soften.

COCONUT PANNA COTTA

Are you surprised to see such a fancy dessert? Don't be! To put it the way David Lebovitz has, if you spend more than 5 minutes making panna cotta, you're taking too long! I like the way you think, David.

I made this one dairy-free and naturally sweetened so that I don't feel badly about eating it for breakfast. And I top it with fruit soaked in honey just because it tastes good. (Honey is acidic and it breaks down the fruit while it rests.) I used figs because summer was in full swing when I perfected this recipe, but mango and raspberries are great here too.

Makes 2 servings

FOR THE FRUIT TOPPING:

4 ripe figs

1 tablespoon honey

FOR THE PANNA COTTA:

1 teaspoon unflavored powdered gelatin

2 teaspoons cold water

1 cup canned, full-fat coconut milk

2 tablespoons honey

⅛ teaspoon fine sea salt

First, make the fruit topping: Wash, trim, and quarter the figs. Cover them with the honey, stir, and let them marinate for at least 1 hour, but up to 1 day.

Next, add the gelatin and cold water to a small bowl. Stir to dissolve the gelatin, then let it rest for 5 minutes.

Meanwhile, in a 2-quart saucepan, heat the coconut milk, honey, and salt. Taste the mixture and adjust it to your taste—more honey, more salt, perhaps a little vanilla extract? It's your call.

Bring the coconut milk almost to a boil—steam will rise quickly from the surface and you might see a few bubbles around the edge of the pan.

Remove the pan from the heat.

Add the gelatin to the coconut mixture and whisk vigorously.

Pour the mixture evenly into two glasses, cover, and let set in the fridge for at least 4 hours or up to 48 hours in advance.

Serve with the honey-soaked figs.

THE 6-INCH >>·· ROUND ·« CAKE PAN

UPSIDE-DOWN BANANA CAKE

As pretty as it is delicious! *Makes one 6-inch cake*

1 small banana, sliced
into ½-inch coins

5 tablespoons unsalted
butter, divided, plus extra
for greasing the pan

3 tablespoons brown sugar

8 teaspoons granulated sugar

1 large egg

½ teaspoon vanilla extract

¼ teaspoon almond extract
(optional)

½ cup all-purpose flour

⅛ teaspoon fine sea salt

¾ teaspoon baking powder

⅓ cup milk

Preheat the oven to 350°F and line the bottom of a 6-inch round cake pan with a circle of parchment paper.

Butter the sides of the pan too.

Place the banana slices in concentric circles in the bottom of the pan.

In a small bowl, combine 2 tablespoons of the butter and the brown sugar. Microwave at full power until melted and bubbling, about 40 seconds. Pour this mixture evenly over the bananas in the pan.

Next, using an electric mixer on medium speed, beat together the remaining 3 tablespoons of butter with the sugar, about 30 seconds.

Add the egg, vanilla, and almond extract (if using) and beat until combined.

Sprinkle the flour, salt, and baking powder evenly over the batter. Beat to combine.

Finally, quickly beat in the milk.

Pour the batter over the bananas in the pan.

Bake for 30 minutes, or until the cake is starting to turn golden brown on the top and a toothpick inserted about halfway comes out clean. The cake will also start to pull away from the edges of the pan and you'll hear the bananas simmering.

Let the cake cool for 10 minutes, invert, and serve.

VERY VANILLA CAKE

I'm pretty boring when it comes to desserts. I'm not even ashamed to admit it. You can call me vanilla, but then you have to serve me vanilla cake. With vanilla frosting. And vanilla ice cream. It's just what I like!

This cake is my ultimate vanilla craving cake. I decorated it with edible chamomile flowers, but they're entirely optional. Who needs decor when you're eating the whole cake by yourself? *Makes one 6-inch cake*

FOR THE CAKE:

6 tablespoons
unsalted butter, softened

½ cup granulated sugar

1 large egg

1 tablespoon vanilla extract

¾ cup all-purpose flour

⅛ teaspoon fine sea salt

¼ teaspoon baking soda

6 tablespoons milk

½ teaspoon apple cider vinegar

FOR THE BUTTERCREAM:

8 tablespoons (1 stick) unsalted butter, at room temperature

2 cups powdered sugar

1 tablespoon vanilla

Splash of milk (only if needed)

Preheat the oven to 350°F and grease a 6-inch round cake pan. Line the bottom with a round of parchment paper.

In a medium-size bowl, beat together the butter and sugar with an electric mixer. Beat very well, about 1 to 2 minutes.

Add the egg and vanilla, and beat until well combined, about 15 seconds.

In a small bowl, whisk together the flour, salt, and baking soda. Add half of this to the batter and beat for just a few seconds before stirring in half of the milk and the vinegar. Continue beating. Add the remaining dry ingredients and beat, then stir in the remaining milk.

Scrape the batter into the pan, smooth out the top, and bake on a small sheet pan for 37 to 39 minutes until an inserted skewer comes out clean.

Let the cake cool on a wire rack in the pan. Carefully remove it from the pan once it has cooled and set it aside.

Then start the buttercream. In a medium-size bowl, beat the butter with an electric mixer until light and fluffy. Add the powdered sugar and vanilla and beat until combined. Add a small splash of milk if the frosting isn't smooth, creamy, and fluffy. If the butter is soft enough, you might not need the milk at all.

MINI SPRINKLES CAKE

In case you were wondering, it's not enough to have a recipe for sprinkles cupcakes. You also need a recipe for a mini sprinkles cake.

    I really like to use this funfetti cake as a mini celebration cake. It's the perfect thing to bring to someone celebrating good news. I've also had friends tell me they make this as a smash cake for their babies. I love that kids and adults alike get excited for sprinkles! *Makes one 6-inch cake*

FOR THE MINI CAKE:

4 tablespoons
unsalted butter, softened

⅓ cup + 2 tablespoons
granulated sugar

1 teaspoon vanilla extract

1 large egg white

⅔ cup all-purpose flour

1 teaspoon baking powder

¼ teaspoon fine sea salt

⅓ cup + 1 tablespoon milk

2½ tablespoons sprinkles

FOR THE FROSTING:

8 tablespoons (1 stick)
unsalted butter, softened

1½ cups powdered sugar

1 to 2 tablespoons milk (or cream)

1 tablespoon sprinkles

First, preheat the oven to 350°F. Spray a 6-inch cake pan with cooking spray. Line the bottom of the pan with parchment paper.

Next, beat together the butter and sugar with an electric mixer until light and fluffy, about 1 to 2 minutes.

Add the vanilla and egg white and beat until well mixed.

Add the flour, baking powder, and salt. Beat for just a few seconds to combine it, and then add all of the milk. Beat until smooth, but do not overmix.

Stir in the sprinkles.

Pour the cake batter into the prepared pan and place it on a baking sheet. Bake for 30 minutes or until an inserted toothpick comes out with only moist crumbs clinging to it.

Let the cake cool slightly before gently tipping it onto a plate—it should come out easily. Peel the parchment paper off the top of the cake.

While the cake is cooling, beat together all of the frosting ingredients except the sprinkles. Stir in the sprinkles last.

Finally, frost the cake, slice, and serve.

If we're being totally honest with each other, my favorite way to eat chocolate is with some fruit. Chocolate and cherries were made for each other. The frosting for this cake is another chance to use up dark cocoa powder if you have it. It tastes great with either regular or dark cocoa, but stick to regular cocoa for the cake part!

Makes one 6-inch cake

BLACK FOREST CAKE

FOR THE CAKE:

½ cup all-purpose flour

5 tablespoons cocoa powder

½ teaspoon baking soda

¼ teaspoon fine sea salt

⅓ cup canola oil

½ cup granulated sugar

⅓ cup full-fat sour cream

1 large egg

½ teaspoon vanilla

1 tablespoon warm water

FOR THE FROSTING:

½ cup heavy cream

¼ cup powdered sugar

2 tablespoons cocoa powder (dark or regular)

FOR GARNISH:

20 fresh dark sweet cherries, pitted

Powdered sugar

Preheat the oven to 350°F and line the bottom a 6-inch round cake pan with a circle of parchment paper. Then spray the pan with cooking spray.

In a small bowl, whisk together the flour, cocoa, baking soda, and salt.

In a medium-size bowl, stir together the oil and sugar with a wooden spoon. Add the sour cream and stir until well blended. Next, add the egg and vanilla. Stir until combined.

Sprinkle half of the flour mixture on the wet mixture. Stir until well blended. Then stir in the water, followed by the remaining flour. Stir until no streaks of flour remain.

Scrape the batter into the cake pan and bake on a baking sheet for 30 minutes. Test with a toothpick to ensure it's done (an underdone cake will sink as it cools).

While the cake is cooling, beat together all of the frosting ingredients with an electric mixer until light and fluffy, like whipped cream. This will take 2 to 3 minutes.

Once the cake is cool, run a knife around the edge and gently tip it out of the pan. Turn it upside down and frost. Refrigerate until ready to serve.

Top with cherries, sprinkle with powdered sugar, and serve.

NEAPOLITAN CAKE

Being a dessert gal, I can never choose just one flavor. I'm so glad it's acceptable to mix flavors at an ice-cream shop these days.

The flavor combo of chocolate, vanilla, and strawberry is one that I fell in love with at an early age, but our love was solidified at In-N-Out burger. If you have an In-N-Out near you, order a Neapolitan shake with your burger next time. You won't regret it.

So, the easiest way for me to get all three flavors into a cake is to take my Very Vanilla Cake (recipe on page 149), top it with a simple strawberry mousse, and decorate it with chocolate shavings.

The strawberry mousse recipe can also be made on its own and served with fresh strawberries on top. It sounds intimidating to make mousse from scratch, but it's really just a heat, stir, and set situation. And I promise, it tastes worlds better than anything from a box. The strawberry flavor really shines through and tastes exactly like a strawberry is meant to taste.

Makes one 6-inch cake

FOR THE CAKE:

1 recipe vanilla cake
(see page 149)

2½ cups sliced fresh strawberries
(frozen will work, but defrost and
slice for accurate measuring)

2 tablespoons granulated sugar

1 tablespoon water

1 teaspoon powdered
unflavored gelatin

⅓ cup heavy whipping cream

Prepare the vanilla cake according to instructions on page 149, and let it cool completely.

In order to get the mousse to set neatly on top, I moved the cake to a 6-inch-deep springform pan, but that's not entirely necessary—you can also frost the cake with the mousse. If you don't have a deep springform pan, line the cake with foil around the edges, giving yourself a 1-inch-high border around the top.

In a small saucepan, add the strawberries and sugar. Turn the heat to medium and cook while stirring frequently, until the strawberries start to break down and a syrup forms around them—about 8 to 10 minutes. Set aside to slightly cool.

(continued)

2 ounces of your favorite chocolate, shaved with a vegetable peeler (or chopped). Or use mini chocolate chips, let's be real.

Meanwhile, add the water to a small bowl and sprinkle the gelatin on top. Stir gently so that all of the gelatin is wet, and let sit for 5 minutes.

Once the gelatin has rested for 5 minutes (also called "blooming"), stir it into the warm strawberry sauce. Then move the strawberry gelatin mixture to a separate bowl and allow it to cool completely.

Once cool, use an immersion stick blender to purée the strawberry gelatin mixture, or place it in a blender to purée until mostly smooth. You will end up with 1 cup of purée.

Next, add the heavy whipping cream to a bowl and beat with an electric mixer on high until soft peaks form. Add the strawberry purée to the cream and continue to beat until light and fluffy, another minute or so, until you have a strawberry mousse.

Pile the strawberry mousse on top of the cake, then move the whole cake to the fridge for about 2 hours to set.

Before serving, shave the chocolate on top, or top with mini chocolate chips.

CRISPY PUMPKIN CAKE

This cake is versatile—make it with all the spices called for and it's reminiscent of a pumpkin spice latte, or make it with just what you have—cinnamon is the only essential spice here. Both versions taste great.

If you're up for the crispy topping, you won't regret it! But honestly, the cake is just as good without it. Without the topping, this cake tastes like my mom's pumpkin bread (and there is no higher compliment). If you're making the crispy topping, feel free to use your favorite nut. Pecans are great here too. *Makes one 6-inch cake*

FOR THE CAKE:

½ cup canned pumpkin purée

3 tablespoons unsalted butter, melted

⅓ cup dark brown sugar

3 tablespoons granulated sugar

1 large egg

¾ cup all-purpose flour

¾ teaspoon ground cinnamon

½ teaspoon ground cloves

½ teaspoon ground ginger

½ teaspoon ground allspice

¼ teaspoon ground cardamom

⅛ teaspoon fine sea salt

¼ teaspoon baking soda

⅛ teaspoon baking powder

1 tablespoon milk

FIRST, MAKE THE CAKE:

Preheat the oven to 350°F and line the bottom of a 6-inch round cake pan with parchment paper. Grease the sides with cooking spray.

In a medium-size bowl, whisk together the pumpkin, melted butter, brown sugar, and granulated sugar. Whisk very well.

Add in the egg and whisk until combined.

In a small bowl, whisk together the flour, spices, salt, baking soda, and baking powder.

Add the dry ingredients to the wet ingredients in two batches, adding the milk in between.

Stir until evenly combined.

Pour in the prepared pan and bake for 30 minutes. Test with a toothpick to ensure it's done.

Let the cake cool completely, leaving it in the pan.

Next, move an oven rack 4 inches below the broiler and preheat the broiler to HIGH.

(continued)

FOR THE CRISPY TOPPING:

2 tablespoons unsalted butter

¼ cup dark brown sugar

⅓ cup chopped hazelnuts

1 teaspoon milk

Pinch of fine sea salt

⅓ cup coconut flakes

NEXT, MAKE THE CRISPY TOPPING:

In a small saucepan, stir together the butter, brown sugar, hazelnuts, milk, and salt.

Bring the mixture to a boil and boil for 1 minute.

Remove from the heat and stir in the coconut flakes.

Pour the mixture evenly over the cake, then place the cake under the broiler. Watch the cake very closely as it browns. It only takes about 40 seconds to brown and crisp completely.

Let the cake cool again before slicing and serving.

Do you need a girlfriend to drink and eat wine with? Yes, I said *eat*.

This chocolate cake has a pronounced wine flavor (but not too much), and the red wine sweet syrup on top is just, well, the icing on the cake. This is another way to use the *dark* cocoa powder in your pantry. Another excellent way!

While I love this dark chocolate cake with its subtle wine flavor, I love the red wine syrup the most. I'm already dreaming up new ways to use it. Would my morning bowl of oatmeal be acceptable? Please say yes.

Makes one 6-inch cake

DARK CHOCOLATE CAKE
+ Red Wine Syrup

FOR THE CAKE:

½ cup all-purpose flour

½ cup granulated sugar

5 tablespoons dark cocoa powder

½ teaspoon baking soda

¼ teaspoon fine sea salt

1 large egg

⅓ cup neutral oil

½ teaspoon vanilla

⅓ cup red wine

FOR THE RED WINE SYRUP:

¾ cup red wine

2 tablespoons granulated sugar

Preheat the oven to 350°F and line a 6-inch cake pan with a small circle of parchment paper. Spray the exposed sides of the pan with cooking spray.

In a small bowl, whisk together the flour, sugar, cocoa powder, baking soda, and salt.

In a separate bowl, whisk together the egg, oil, and vanilla.

Add the wet ingredients to the dry and stir gently until mixed, adding the wine about halfway through.

Pour the batter into the pan and bake on a baking sheet for 30 minutes, or until an inserted toothpick comes out mostly clean, with a few crumbs clinging to it. If you underbake the cake, it will sink as it cools.

Let the cake cool in the pan for 15 minutes.

Meanwhile, make the wine syrup: Combine the wine and sugar in a small saucepan and bring to a boil. Boil until reduced to 2 to 3 tablespoons, about 15 minutes.

Remove the cake from the pan and place on a serving plate.

Slice and serve with the red wine syrup drizzled on top.

CHOCOLATE TRUFFLE CAKE

I am *allllllll* about an easy dessert. And if it only has three ingredients, even better! You can stir this cake together in 10 minutes flat and pop it in the oven.

When it comes out of the oven, it will look a little plain and flat, but a sprinkling of powdered sugar and some raspberries will fix it right up. If you need to take it a step further, a simple raspberry sauce on top would offer the perfect counterbalance to the rich chocolate.

I use a mini springform pan that measures 6 inches across, but a regular 6-inch pan would work too. Use a flexible spatula to help remove the cake from the pan. *Makes one 6-inch cake*

6 tablespoons unsalted butter

6 tablespoons semisweet chocolate, chopped

3 large eggs

Preheat the oven to 325°F and wrap the bottom of a 6-inch springform pan with two layers of foil. Ensure the foil comes up on the sides—we're trying to prevent any water from entering the cake when we bake it in a water bath.

Place the springform pan inside an 8-inch square pan. We're going to bake this cake in a water bath, and the square pan will hold the water.

Bring 2 cups of water to boil in a kettle.

In a medium-size microwave-safe bowl, combine the butter and chopped chocolate.

Heat the chocolate mixture in the microwave on 50 percent power for about 1 minute, pausing after 30 seconds to stir.

When the bowl comes out of the microwave, the chocolate may not be melted all the way. Just let it rest on the counter and stir after a few minutes—then it should be melted completely.

While the chocolate is melting, beat the eggs with an electric mixer on high speed until pale yellow, creamy, and doubled in volume. This will take about 3 to 4 minutes.

When the chocolate is smooth, pour ⅓ of it into the beaten eggs and carefully fold it together. (Proper folding technique is down the middle with a spatula, sweeping around the sides after each turn.)

Add another third of the chocolate mixture and keep folding.

Finally, fold in the last of the chocolate.

Scrape the mixture into the springform pan.

Carefully pour the boiling water into the square pan. The water will come about halfway up on the sides of the springform pan.

Carefully move the pan to the oven on the middle rack and bake for 20 minutes.

Check the cake after 20 minutes—the surface should be dull and have a slight crust. If not, return the pan to the oven for 5 minutes.

When the cake is done, let it cool completely in the water bath.

Then, carefully remove the springform pan from the water and place it in the fridge to chill for at least 4 hours before slicing, sprinkling with powdered sugar and raspberries, and serving.

GINGERBREAD CAKE
+ Lemon Glaze

Ahhh, gingerbread, chai, and warm spices—they're kinda my thing. This is probably because I'm always cold. My pantry is always stocked with spices. But I should admit: I don't just make this spicy sweet gingerbread cake when the weather is chilly. I think the bright lemon glaze on top makes it perfectly acceptable for warm months too. *Makes one 6-inch cake*

FOR THE CAKE:

¾ cup + 2 tablespoons all-purpose flour

1½ teaspoon ground ginger

1 teaspoon cinnamon

Pinch of ground cloves

⅛ teaspoon fine sea salt

½ teaspoon baking soda

¼ cup canola oil

2 tablespoons unsalted butter, melted

1 large egg

¼ cup brown sugar

3 tablespoons molasses

FOR THE GLAZE:

Juice of ½ lemon

¾ cup powdered sugar

Preheat the oven to 350°F and thoroughly grease a 6-inch round cake pan.

In a small bowl, whisk together the flour, ginger, cinnamon, cloves, salt, and baking soda.

In a separate bowl, whisk together the oil, melted butter, egg, brown sugar, and molasses. Whisk very well until homogenized; it will take a while to blend the egg and molasses together.

Stir the wet and dry ingredients together, then pour the mixture into the prepared cake pan.

Bake for 30 to 33 minutes until an inserted toothpick comes out clean. The cake may have a slight divot in the center.

Let the cake cool in the pan and then tilt it out onto a serving plate.

Whisk together the lemon juice and powdered sugar to make the glaze. Pour it over the cake and serve.

APPLE TARTE TATIN

My husband's favorite dessert is apple pie, and you would think that having killer deep-dish apple pie and apple crisp recipes up my sleeve would be enough to cure his cravings. When you love apples as much as he does, any iteration of apples + sugar + buttery crust is welcome . . . I've even seen him chase apple pie with another apple dessert. He might have a problem.

I like to plan a date night at home for two, cook a French-inspired dinner, and then bring this beauty to the table for dessert. If you can flip it out of the pan at the table (without burning yourself), you're going to impress! If you burn yourself, well, that just means you get to eat both servings, okay?

The pastry part of this recipe is a homemade puff pastry. You can defrost store-bought puff pastry from the freezer for an even easier version.

One more note on apples: Since we're using a small, 6-inch pan, it's nice to find small apples. I have the best luck with tiny, organic, local apples. They may be wimpy in size, but I promise they'll deliver on flavor. *Makes one 6-inch cake*

FOR THE PASTRY:

½ cup all-purpose flour

⅛ teaspoon fine sea salt

5 tablespoons cold unsalted butter, cubed

2½ tablespoons ice water

FOR THE REST:

1 small apple, peeled and cut into 8 pieces

⅓ cup granulated sugar

Pinch of fine sea salt

3 tablespoons unsalted butter, diced

2 teaspoons fresh lemon juice

First, make the pastry: In a medium-size bowl, add the flour and salt. Stir to mix.

Next, add the cubed butter to the flour bowl. Using a pastry blender or two knives, cut the butter into the dough. It will be very crumbly—you're on the right track when the butter is in uniform pieces about the size of peas.

Next, make a hole in the center of the dough and pour in the water. Using a fork, stir to combine the dough.

Flour a cutting board and place the dough on top. Pat it into a rough square. You will still see chunks of butter and it might seem too dry, but do not add extra water. The dough will come together with each roll.

Flour a rolling pin and roll the dough out into a rectangle about 5 inches long.

Fold the bottom third of the dough over the middle of the dough. Fold the upper third of the dough on top of the middle too. Rotate the dough one-quarter turn and repeat. Use additional flour as needed to prevent the dough from sticking.

Roll out the dough again, fold it, turn it, and repeat at least six or seven times.

When done, wrap the dough in plastic wrap and chill for at least an hour, or overnight. The dough may be frozen for up to 2 months; thaw in the refrigerator before using.

Next, preheat the oven to 425°F. Have your cake pan ready on the side.

Peel and core the apples. Slice the apple into eight equal-sized pieces. Set aside.

In a small skillet over medium-low heat, add the sugar in an even layer. Let it melt without stirring until it's bubbling and fully dissolved. Keep an eye on it—it can burn! To evenly distribute the sugar during cooking, gently tilt the skillet—do not stir with a spoon. If any sugar crystals get on the edge of the skillet and won't melt back down, use a pastry brush dipped in water to nudge them back in.

Once the sugar is turning a light golden color, add the butter a few pieces at a time. Be careful—it will splatter!

Once all of the butter is incorporated, add the apples to the skillet. Cook the apples in the caramel sauce, stirring occasionally, until the caramel turns a deep amber brown. It will thicken to the consistency of maple syrup.

Remove the apples from the skillet, reserving the caramel sauce in the skillet, and arrange them prettily in the cake pan, cut side up. Use one piece in the center to "anchor" the design, and arrange the slices around it. Cram the apples in tightly because they will shrink as they bake.

Next, add the salt and lemon juice to the reserved caramel sauce in the skillet. Swirl to stir. Pour this mixture evenly over the apples in the cake pan.

Remove the puff pastry from the fridge and flour a surface. Roll the pastry out to get a 6-inch circle of dough. Move the dough disk to the pan to cover the apples. Tuck the excess pastry down toward the bottom of the pan.

Move the pan to a small baking sheet and bake for 20 minutes. When done, the surface of the puff pastry should look dry.

Let the tarte rest in the pan for 5 to 10 minutes. Then place a serving plate on top of it and, using oven mitts, flip the skillet to turn out the tarte. If any apples slide around, move them back into place. And there you have it!

It's not the holidays without my mom's fudge. Her recipe makes a giant pan of it, and no matter how many people share it, everyone always eats too much. That's just the way it goes with fudge. It's super sweet, soft, and craveable.

I make a small batch of her fudge in a cake pan, and when sliced like a cake into eight pieces, it proves to be just enough fudge for two people.

The base of this fudge is just two ingredients: sweetened condensed milk and chopped chocolate. Make it plain, or make variations with almond extract, orange zest, etc. Here we have two versions you can try: chocolate and orange creamsicle. *Makes one 6-inch cake*

TWO-INGREDIENT FUDGE, TWO WAYS

FOR THE CHOCOLATE VERSION:

½ of a 14-ounce can of sweetened condensed milk

9 ounces chopped chocolate (semisweet chocolate chips or your favorite chocolate bar)

½ teaspoon almond extract (optional)

Slivered almonds, for topping

FOR THE ORANGE CREAMSICLE VERSION:

½ of a 14-ounce can of sweetened condensed milk

9 ounces chopped white chocolate

2 large oranges, zested

FOR THE CHOCOLATE VERSION:

Line a 6-inch round cake pan with foil and spray lightly with cooking spray. (I use coconut oil cooking spray.)

In a small saucepan over VERY low heat, add the condensed milk. Stir in the chocolate chips. Slowly let the chocolate melt into the condensed milk, stirring constantly to prevent the chocolate from getting too hot and seizing.

Once everything is smooth and melted, stir in the almond extract. Taste and add more, if you like.

Pour the fudge into the prepared pan, and sprinkle the slivered almonds on top, pressing them lightly so they stick.

Place the pan in the fridge and chill for at least 4 hours.

Lift the fudge out of the pan using the foil, then cut into slices and serve.

FOR THE ORANGE CREAMSICLE VERSION:

Follow the steps for the chocolate version, but substitute white chocolate chips for the semisweet ones, and substitute orange zest for the almond extract.

THE
8-INCH
SQUARE PAN

SMALL CARROT CAKE
+ Caramel Cream Cheese Frosting

We eat a lot of carrot cake in my house. Over the years, I've scaled it down to serve two in a small, round cake pan, and I've even scaled it down into two ramekins. But the truth is, there are times when we need a little more than that. We'll never need a giant three-layer one (well, maybe once a year at Easter), but a slightly larger 8-inch square cake is perfect for a small dinner party.

The other thing I love about this cake is that it comes together so easily, with just two bowls and a wooden spoon—no mixer required. In the case of this cake, a mixer would whip too much air into it and it would sink as it cooled.

The best type of carrots to use for this cake are freshly grated ones. The carrots sold pregrated at the store are too big. To hand-grate the carrots, use the large holes on your box grater. *Makes one 8-inch square cake*

FOR THE CAKE:

½ cup neutral oil (like canola or grapeseed)

1 cup granulated sugar

2 large eggs, beaten

½ teaspoon vanilla extract

½ cup canned crushed pineapple, drained

1 cup freshly grated carrot

1 cup all-purpose flour

½ teaspoon baking powder

¾ teaspoon baking soda

½ teaspoon ground cinnamon

Preheat the oven to 350°F and line an 8-inch square pan with parchment paper on all sides by laying one piece of paper one way and then another piece the opposite way.

In a large bowl, stir the oil and sugar together with a wooden spoon (do not use a mixer). Add the eggs, vanilla, pineapple, and carrots.

In a separate bowl, stir together the flour, baking powder, baking soda, and cinnamon.

Sprinkle the dry ingredients over the wet and stir until combined.

Pour the batter into the prepared pan and bake for 33 to 36 minutes until nicely golden brown and starting to pull away from the edges of the pan.

Let the cake cool completely.

FOR THE CARAMEL CREAM CHEESE FROSTING:

¾ cup caramel bits
(or chopped caramel candies)

8 ounces cream cheese, softened

½ cup powdered sugar

1 teaspoon vanilla extract

As the cake cools, whip together the frosting. First, melt the caramel bits in the microwave with a splash of water. Set aside.

With an electric mixer, beat the cream cheese and powdered sugar until light and fluffy. Stir in the caramel and vanilla.

Frost the cake with the caramel cream cheese frosting and serve.

Now that I've been blessed with a daughter, I have a serious need for pink cakes in my life. We've only had one birthday party for Camille so far, and I chickened out on giving her real sugar. I made her the Maple Syrup Cupcakes on page 103.

But as she gets older, I know I'm not going to be able to fool her anymore, and I also know hot pink cakes will be demanded.

I may give in on the sugar, but I'm a woman of conviction when it comes to food coloring, and I will not rely on it to make her pink dreams come true. Instead, I've found that frozen fruit makes frosting the most lovely shade of hot pink. Do I get my mom medal now? I've been waiting on that thing for months! *Makes one 8-inch square cake*

HOT PINK RASPBERRY CAKE
(for Camille)

FOR THE CAKE:

7 tablespoons unsalted butter, at room temperature

1 cup granulated sugar

2 large eggs

1 teaspoon vanilla

1 cup all-purpose flour

1 teaspoon baking powder

⅓ cup milk

FOR THE FROSTING:

4 ounces cream cheese, softened

3 tablespoons unsalted butter, at room temperature

1 cup powdered sugar

½ cup frozen raspberries, defrosted, with their juice

Preheat the oven to 325°F and line the bottom of an 8-inch square pan with a piece of parchment paper. Spray the exposed sides of the lined pan with cooking spray.

In a medium-size bowl, using an electric mixer on medium speed, beat together the butter and sugar until light and fluffy, about 1 to 2 minutes.

Add the eggs and vanilla and beat until just combined.

In a small bowl, whisk the flour and baking powder together. Have the milk ready on the side.

Add half of the dry ingredients to the batter and stir until combined. Add half of the milk and stir again. Repeat with the remaining flour and milk.

Pour the batter into the prepared pan and bake for 28 to 32 minutes, or until a wooden toothpick inserted into the center comes out clean.

Let the cake cool completely in the pan.

Run a knife around the edge and gently tip out the cake.

Slice the cake in half to make two layers and set aside.

While the cake is cooling, beat together all ingredients for the frosting with an electric mixer on high speed. Beat for 1 to 2 minutes, until the frosting is light and fluffy.

Place one-half of the cake on a serving dish and top with about one-third of the frosting. Spread evenly and top with the remaining cake half to make one long rectangular cake.

Spread the remaining pink frosting on the top and sides of the cake.

Slice into five triangles (or two big rectangles!) and serve.

S'MORES CAKE

If you can make my standard chocolate cake in an 8-inch square pan (which you totally can), then you can cut it in half, stack it, and make a mini s'mores layer cake for two. It's almost as exciting as the toasted marshmallow and graham cracker crumb filling! *Makes one 8-inch square cake*

FOR THE CAKE:

1 large egg

½ cup milk

¼ cup canola oil

2 teaspoons vanilla extract

1 cup all-purpose flour

1 cup granulated sugar

½ cup unsweetened cocoa powder

¾ teaspoon baking powder

¾ teaspoon baking soda

½ teaspoon fine sea salt

½ cup hot coffee

FOR THE REST:

¼ pound (2 sticks) unsalted butter, at room temperature

1½ cups powdered sugar

½ cup unsweetened cocoa powder

1 teaspoon vanilla

Pinch of fine sea salt

1 to 2 tablespoons leftover hot coffee

½ bag jumbo marshmallows, snipped in half with kitchen scissors

10 graham cracker sheets, crumbled

FIRST, MAKE THE CAKE:

Preheat the oven to 350°F and line an 8-inch square pan with parchment paper.

In a large measuring cup (or bowl), whisk together the egg, milk, canola oil, and vanilla.

In a medium-size bowl, whisk together the flour, sugar, cocoa powder, baking powder, baking soda, and salt.

Slowly pour the egg mixture into the dry ingredients, followed by the hot coffee.

Stir until the batter is smooth and lump-free. (Ensure there are no lumps of flour at the bottom of the bowl!)

Pour the batter into the prepared pan and bake for 36 to 40 minutes, or until a toothpick tester comes out with only moist crumbs clinging to it. The cake will begin to pull away from the edges of the pan when it's done.

Let the cake cool completely in the pan.

Lift the cake out of the pan using the parchment paper as handles.

Slice the cake in half down the middle.

Place one-half of the cake on a serving plate.

NEXT, MAKE THE FROSTING:

In a medium-size bowl, beat together the butter, powdered sugar, cocoa powder, vanilla, and salt with an electric mixer on high speed. Stream in the coffee, as needed, to make a fluffy, spreadable frosting.

Add a small scoop of frosting on top of the cake half on the plate and spread it to the edges.

Cover the frosting with an even layer of marshmallow halves. Fill the surface completely.

Use a kitchen torch to lightly toast the marshmallows.

Sprinkle about one-third of the graham cracker crumbs on top of the toasted marshmallows.

Top the cake with the other half. Add a thicker layer of frosting this time and top that with another layer of marshmallows.

Torch the marshmallows until they're as crispy/chewy/burnt/toasted as you like them. It's your cake!

Sprinkle graham cracker crumbs on top of the marshmallows.

Spread the remaining frosting on the sides of the cake. You're only going to have enough for a thin coat, but that's okay. This cake is rich!

MINI CHOCOLATE LAYER CAKES

If you can't tell by now, I love making mini layer cakes. They look so special and are so easy to pull off. You can make two mini chocolate layer cakes if you bake a small chocolate cake in an 8-inch square brownie pan. Use a cookie cutter to cut out four "layers" from the 8-inch cake, then hold it all together with rich chocolate frosting. This recipe uses the same base cake as the S'mores Cake on the previous page.

There will be leftover cake "scraps" after you cut out your cake layers. You can mix these with the remaining frosting to make cake balls!

I also want to mention that these are the kind of cakes that you cannot frost completely. Because the edges of the cake are raw from being cut, the frosting sticks to the cake crumbs something fierce, making it nearly impossible to frost. If you are a super skilled baker, you could try making a crumb coat first—if that works for you, please come teach me how to do it!

Makes 2 mini cakes + 6 cake truffles

(*continued*)

1 recipe chocolate cake (see page 176)

8 tablespoons (1 stick)
unsalted butter, softened

2½ cups powdered sugar

¼ cup unsweetened cocoa powder

2 teaspoons vanilla extract

2 to 4 teaspoons milk
(as needed, for consistency)

Prepare the chocolate cake according to the instructions on page 176, and let it cool completely.

While the cake is cooling, beat together the butter, sugar, and cocoa powder using an electric mixer on medium speed.

Add the vanilla and 2 teaspoons of milk. Use additional milk, if needed, to make the frosting come together smoothly.

To make the mini cake layers, cut out four cake circles using a 3-inch-wide cookie cutter.

The cakes may be uneven—if so, use a knife to level them off.

Get out two serving plates and put one cake layer on each. To each one, add a big dollop of frosting. Spread the frosting almost to the edge.

Put the remaining two cake layers on top of the frosted ones and top the cakes with more frosting.

Finally, crumble the cake scraps left in the pan. Combine the cake crumbs with the remaining frosting and roll into cake truffles!

LEMON MATCHA CAKE ROLL

Oh, matcha. My one true love. I have completely fallen for matcha over the past few years. I'm not much of a coffee drinker, and besides espresso powder in my chocolate desserts, you'll hardly find me using coffee in my baking.

If that makes you sad, please forgive me. I hope this mini lemon cake roll stuffed to the brim with matcha-flavored whipped cream will help ease any tension between the two of us. *Makes one 8-inch roll cake*

FOR THE CAKE:

5 tablespoons all-purpose flour

½ teaspoon baking powder

½ teaspoon cornstarch

3 tablespoons whole milk (NOT skim or 1%)

1 tablespoon unsalted butter

5 tablespoons granulated sugar

2 large eggs, at room temperature

1 large lemon, zested

FOR THE WHIPPED CREAM:

⅓ cup heavy whipping cream

1 tablespoon matcha powder

½ cup powdered sugar, plus extra for decorating

EASY TIP: *If you are going to store this cake before serving, add 1 teaspoon of gelatin to the cream before whipping it.*

The only pan that will work for this recipe is a *metal* 8-inch square pan with sharp corners (sorry, cake rolls are finicky). Do not use ceramic or silicone bakeware.

First, preheat the oven to 350°F. Then, trace the bottom of the pan on a piece of parchment paper, and then cut out the square. The parchment paper should fit exactly in the bottom of the pan, with no overhang whatsoever. (Any bumps or gaps in the paper will allow batter underneath and ruin your cake!) Place the parchment paper square in the bottom of the pan. Do NOT grease the pan.

In a small bowl, sift the flour, baking powder, and cornstarch together. Sift it into another bowl again, and then finally back into the first one for a total of three sifts. Be careful not to lose any flour in the process! Set aside.

Next, melt the butter and milk in a small dish in the microwave at full power for 20 seconds or so. Leave it in the microwave (you'll reheat it one more time).

Finally, in a medium-size bowl, combine the sugar and eggs. Beat with an electric mixer on high speed until it has the consistency of whipped cream. This will take

(continued)

5 to 10 minutes; the older, smaller hand mixers require more time to whip.

Add one-third of the flour mixture to the egg mixture and gently fold in with a rubber spatula. Add the rest of the flour in two batches, gently folding in both times.

Reheat the milk and butter mixture in the microwave for another 15 seconds before pouring it into the batter and folding it in.

Add the lemon zest. Fold everything together long enough to ensure the mixture is homogenous.

Pour the mixture into the prepared pan and bake for 19 to 21 minutes, or until a toothpick comes out clean.

Let the cake cool in the pan on a wire rack for 2 minutes, then run a knife around the edge of the pan to release the cake.

Gently tip the cake out onto a clean kitchen towel. Peel off the parchment paper (it's okay if a very thin layer of cake sticks to it). Leave the rough side of the cake facing up.

Now you're going to roll the cake. Don't be afraid. Move quickly and with confidence! You got this! Start by using your fingers to roll the first inch of the cake over on itself, before using your whole hands to roll the whole cake at once. Once it's rolled up, do not unroll it until it's completely cool. Even if there are a few cracks, do not worry—you'll sprinkle the whole thing with powdered sugar to hide them.

While the cake cools, whip together the cream, matcha, and powdered sugar. Beat until light and fluffy. Cover and chill in the fridge to firm it up slightly.

When the cake is cool, unroll, spread with the whipped cream, and roll back up.

If you don't want to serve it right away, wrap it in plastic wrap and chill until ready to serve.

To serve, sprinkle powdered sugar all over the top of the roll and slice.

I figured we all need a good zucchini cake in our files. This is especially true when a summer vacation coincides with an epic period of zucchini production. Yes, I'm speaking from experience here.

When I think about vegetables, all I think about is how to get more of them into my kid. Cake is an obvious choice, but like always, when I bake for her I reach for more natural, unrefined sweeteners. I used coconut sugar for this cake and maple syrup for the frosting. The frosting isn't as sweet as typical cream cheese frosting, but I like it better. (If you want to, add ½ cup of powdered sugar.)

After you grate the zucchini, place it on several sheets of paper towel, let it rest for about 5 minutes, and then try to squeeze as much moisture from it as you can by pressing down on it. *Makes one 8-inch square cake*

ZUCCHINI CAKE

FOR THE CAKE:

1¼ cups all-purpose flour

2 teaspoons ground cinnamon

½ teaspoon ground nutmeg

½ teaspoon ground ginger

½ teaspoon fine sea salt

½ teaspoon baking powder

½ teaspoon baking soda

½ cup vegetable oil

½ cup unsweetened applesauce

1 teaspoon vanilla

2 eggs

1 cup coconut sugar

1 cup shredded zucchini, drained and patted dry

FOR THE FROSTING:

8 ounces cream cheese

¼ cup maple syrup

½ teaspoon vanilla

Preheat the oven to 350°F. Butter or spray an 8-inch square baking pan with nonstick cooking spray and set aside.

In a bowl, combine flour, spices, salt, baking powder, and baking soda.

In a separate bowl, combine oil, applesauce, vanilla, eggs, and sugar. Add to the dry ingredients and mix well.

Add the shredded zucchini and stir until thoroughly combined.

Pour the batter into the prepared pan.

Bake for 30 to 35 minutes or until a toothpick inserted near the center comes out clean. Cool on a wire rack.

Meanwhile, in a small bowl, beat the cream cheese, vanilla, and maple syrup until smooth and creamy.

When the cake is completely cool, frost it, and serve.

CHAI-POACHED PEARS AND CREAM

This is my favorite dessert to make for myself when I want something sweet, but I want to be "good." Baked pears are so soft and sweet, it's almost like you're enjoying creamy custard. (I said *almost*.) And you know me: I believe chai spices make everything better. Use any combination of spices you prefer—a cinnamon stick being the only "absolute must" in this recipe. *Makes 6 poached halves*

½ cup maple syrup

½ cup water

1 cinnamon stick, broken

1 star anise

2 cardamom pods, crushed

2 cloves

2 black peppercorns

3 large pears

Vanilla ice cream, for serving

Preheat the oven to 400°F. In a square baking dish, combine the maple syrup, water, and spices. Whisk very well to combine, and crush the spices as needed to extract flavor.

Peel and slice the pears in half, scooping out the seeds with a small spoon or melon baller.

Place the pears in the baking dish and stir gently to coat in the maple-spice mixture. Use a spoon to help coat the pears.

Turn all the pears cut-side down and cover the pan with foil.

Bake for 20 minutes.

Remove the foil after 20 minutes, give the pears a quick stir to coat, and bake for another 10 minutes. The sauce will thicken and become syrupy.

Remove the pears from the baking dish and strain the syrup.

Serve the pears warm, drizzled with the syrup and ice cream on the side.

Here's the thing about lemon bars: I love them every which way. I love them thick or thin. I love them with a crème brûlée crust (catch that recipe in my first book). I love them homemade or from a bakery. I love them hot or cold. But most of all, I love them with a gingersnap crust. Not only is it easier to smash cookies for a crust than it is to make a standard shortbread crust, but lemon and ginger were made for each other. Like dogs and peanut butter. Like yoga pants and Netflix. Like me and lemon desserts. *Makes 6 lemon bars*

EASIEST LEMON BARS

3 cups small gingersnap cookies
(about 35 two-inch cookies)

2 tablespoons
unsalted butter, melted

3 (10-ounce) jars of lemon curd

3 tablespoons fresh lemon juice

2 teaspoons plain,
unflavored gelatin

Powdered sugar (for serving)

Preheat the oven to 350°F and line an 8-inch square pan with parchment paper, leaving enough on the ends to use as handles. Lightly spray the exposed sides with cooking spray.

Place the cookies in a small food processor and pulse until finely ground. Alternately, crush them in a plastic bag with a rolling pin.

Stir the melted butter into the cookie crumbs. Press the gingersnap crust into the pan in an even layer.

Bake for 12 minutes.

Move the pan to the fridge to cool completely.

Next, add all of the lemon curd into a big bowl and have a whisk ready.

In a small (nonmetal/nonreactive) saucepan, add 2 tablespoons of the lemon juice.

Sprinkle the gelatin over the top and stir gently to combine. Let it rest and bloom for 5 minutes.

Then, add the remaining tablespoon of lemon juice and whisk in thoroughly.

Turn the heat to medium-low and keep whisking until the mixture is completely dissolved (it will be 100 percent liquid, no clumps).

Add the gelatin mixture to the lemon curd and whisk very well to combine.

Pour the lemon curd mixture over the crust and place back in the fridge to set for at least 4 hours before slicing and serving.

CHOCOLATE CHIP COOKIE STICKS

What's easier than making chocolate chip cookies? Making chocolate chip cookie sticks! These babes are pressed flat into a pan all at once and are sliced after baking. And that's great for someone like me who can never find her dang cookie scoop.

I use mini chocolate chips in this recipe because it equates to more chocolate per bite. I haven't exactly done the math on it, but when I look at the dough, the space between chocolate chips is a lot smaller. And that makes me a lot happier. *Makes 1 dozen cookie sticks*

8 tablespoons (1 stick) unsalted butter, softened

½ cup powdered sugar

2 tablespoons honey

1 teaspoon vanilla extract

1 cup all-purpose flour

¾ teaspoon fine sea salt

½ cup mini chocolate chips

Preheat the oven to 350°F and line the bottom of an 8-inch square pan with parchment paper. Lightly grease the edges to ensure the cookies don't stick.

In a bowl, beat together the butter, powdered sugar, and honey with an electric mixer on medium speed. Beat very well until fluffy, about 45 seconds.

Add the vanilla and beat until combined.

Sprinkle the flour and salt evenly on top of the butter mixture and beat until combined.

Finally, add the mini chips and stir until evenly mixed.

Press the dough flat into the pan (you might have to lightly flour your hands to help it spread).

Bake for 20 minutes or until the edges start to lightly brown.

Let cool for 5 minutes, remove from pan, slice, and serve. (Using a pizza wheel is the best way to cut these.)

If celery + onions + bell peppers are the holy trinity in Cajun cooking, then chocolate + peanut butter + coconut is the holy trinity in my kitchen. Anytime these three are together, the results are delicious.

When I came up with this recipe, I was craving one of those oatmeal squares stuffed with chocolate. You know the ones. But I wanted a crispier, no-bake, easy version that I could keep in the fridge for those 3 p.m. chocolate cravings. I usually make these with coconut sugar because it somehow makes me feel less guilty, but brown sugar is a great substitute. And if you can believe it, butter is an even more delicious substitute than coconut oil, but the choice is yours. *Makes 1 dozen bars*

NO-BAKE CHOCOLATE GRANOLA BARS

2¼ cup rolled oats

½ cup unsweetened coconut flakes

Pinch of fine sea salt

½ cup coconut sugar

¾ cup coconut oil

¾ cup creamy peanut butter

1 cup chopped dark chocolate

Line an 8-inch sqaure pan with aluminum foil that covers all sides.

In a small food processor, add the oats, coconut flakes, and the pinch of salt. Pulse about seven or eight times until the oats are broken down a bit. Place in a large bowl.

Next, melt the coconut sugar into the coconut oil. Use a whisk to combine the two very well.

Pour the coconut oil mixture over the oats and stir to combine.

Divide the oat mixture in half and press half of it firmly into the bottom of the pan.

Next, in a microwave-safe bowl, combine the peanut butter and dark chocolate. Heat at 50 percent power, stopping every 30 seconds to stir. Remove the bowl from the microwave before everything is totally melted, about 90 seconds total. Let rest on the counter, stirring occasionally until smooth.

Pour the chocolate–peanut butter mixture on top of the crust, then sprinkle the remaining oat mixture over that.

Cover and refrigerate for at least 4 hours, or until firm.

Store these bars in the fridge.

BEST EVER JAM BARS

I can be a bit of a jam hoarder. It's one of my favorite things to buy at farmers' markets, and it's my favorite gift to receive. (Take note!)

A lot of jam bars are too soggy for me. It's just the nature of the beast—baking sugary jam in between layers of soft batter. But I fixed the problem for us! A little almond meal (just ground almonds—you can make it yourself in a food processor) and coconut flakes in the batter make for a jam bar with a crisp crust and a molten jam center.

I'm not even afraid to say it: these are the best jam bars ever. *Makes 6 bars*

½ cup almond meal

1 cup all-purpose flour

½ cup unsweetened coconut flakes

¼ teaspoon fine sea salt

¼ teaspoon baking powder

9 tablespoons unsalted butter, softened, plus extra for greasing the pan

¼ cup dark brown sugar

½ cup granulated sugar

1 large egg white

Heaping ½ cup of your favorite jam

Preheat the oven to 350°F and butter an 8-inch square baking dish.

In a medium-size bowl, whisk together the almond meal, flour, coconut, salt, and baking powder.

In a separate bowl, cream the softened butter with the sugars until light and fluffy. Add the egg white and beat until combined.

Add the dry ingredients to the wet and beat until combined.

Spread half of the dough onto the bottom of the baking dish, using your fingers to press it into an even layer.

Spread the jam over the surface (if you leave a half-centimeter border, the bars won't stick to the pan as badly).

Top the jam with the remaining dough, using your fingers to make big crumbles of dough.

Bake for 30 to 32 minutes, until the edges start to turn deeply golden brown.

Let cool in the pan, then cut and serve.

Toffee is one of those things that I used to be too intimidated to make at home. I've had a few failures, I will admit. When I figured out that I could make toffee based on watching the sugar change color instead of using a thermometer, I was a changed woman. I make this often over the holidays, but it's welcome any time of year. *Makes one 8-inch square of toffee*

EASY TOFFEE

½ cup whole almonds, toasted

8 tablespoons (1 stick) unsalted butter, plus extra for greasing the pan

½ cup granulated sugar

¼ teaspoon fine sea salt

1 cup chocolate chips

¼ cup sliced almonds

First, line the 8-inch square pan with foil and butter the foil generously.

Evenly sprinkle the whole almonds across the foil.

Next, in a 2-quart saucepan, add the butter, sugar, and salt. Turn the heat to medium and cook, occasionally stirring, until the mixture turns a peanut butter color, about 8 to 10 minutes.

Immediately remove the mixture from the heat and pour it over the almonds in the pan.

Then immediately distribute the chocolate chips on top of the toffee. Let rest for 1 minute before using a spatula to smooth the surface of the chocolate. (It's magic!)

Finally, sprinkle the sliced almonds on top.

Let the mixture cool in the pan, about 3 to 4 hours, before breaking into pieces and sharing.

INDIVIDUAL PEACH CRISPS

Dessert is nearly always infinitely better when its personal sized.

You want to seek out freestone peaches for this recipe. Freestone peaches easily twist open when sliced, as opposed to clingstone peaches, which are nearly impossible to twist apart into two usable peach halves.

Makes 6 baked peach halves

3 large almost-ripe freestone peaches (still slightly firm to the touch)

7 tablespoons cold unsalted butter, diced

¾ cup brown sugar

¾ cup rolled oats

½ cup all-purpose flour

1 teaspoon cinnamon

¼ teaspoon fine sea salt

Vanilla ice cream, for serving

Preheat the oven to 425°F and have ready an 8-inch square dish.

Slice the peaches in half, twist open, and remove the pits.

In a small bowl, combine all remaining ingredients. Use your fingers or a pastry blender to work the dough together. It will be firm and very easy to clump together in your hand.

Divide the dough in half by eye, then portion it out between all six of the peach halves. Pile the dough on top of each peach half, packing it together firmly.

Bake for about 15 minutes, until the crisp topping is golden brown and the peaches are starting to soften.

Serve warm. Ice cream optional (but then again, it's not).

Oh, this cake. It's not to be missed. It's a crisp, buttery crust with a gooey vanilla filling and a topping that shatters like the first bite of a glazed dough-nut. I'm not overselling this, I promise.

Gooey butter cake (when not made from a cake mix, and thus approxi-mately a thousand times better) is two wet batters poured on top of each other and baked. There are yeast versions out there, which I love and adore, but this is my favorite.

If you want to take it up a notch (and dirty another dish), try browning the butter first. *Makes one 8-inch square cake*

DOUGHNUT GOOEY BUTTER CAKE

FOR THE BOTTOM LAYER:

6 tablespoons
unsalted butter, melted

½ cup granulated sugar

½ cup brown sugar

2 large eggs

¾ teaspoon fine sea salt

1½ cups all-purpose flour

2 teaspoons baking powder

FOR THE TOP LAYER:

8 ounces cream cheese, softened

6 tablespoons brown sugar

2 large eggs

1 tablespoon vanilla extract

3½ cups powdered sugar,
plus extra for serving

Preheat the oven to 350°F and line an 8-inch square baking pan one direction with parchment paper ("one direction" means the paper covers the bottom and only two sides of the pan). Lightly spray the exposed sides of the pan with cooking spray.

Next, make the bottom layer of the cake. In a medium-size bowl, whisk together the melted butter and sugars.

Add the eggs and salt, and whisk well to combine. Finally, add the flour and baking powder.

Scoop the mixture into the prepared pan and press flat with your hands. It's a bit sticky—flour your fingers to help spread it evenly.

Then wipe out the bowl and start making the top layer of the cake. Add the cream cheese and brown sugar. Beat with an electric mixer on medium speed until light and fluffy, about 1 minute. Add the eggs and vanilla. Beat until combined. Finally, add the powdered sugar and beat until well mixed and smooth.

Pour the top layer onto the bottom layer.

Bake for 50 to 55 minutes, until the center only has a slight jiggle. Don't overbake (or it won't be gooey).

Let cool completely, then refrigerate or freeze until firm enough to cut.

Sprinkle with powdered sugar and serve.

Any Leftover Eggs?

Why not use up any spare egg yolks or whites from these recipes by making another sweet and simple treat?

Recipes to use up an extra egg yolk:

Recipes to use up an extra egg white:

Acknowledgments

Many thanks to my team at Countryman Press who keep insisting they can make books out of my wild recipe ideas. I absolutely love working with you. Thanks for making things so easy on me and giving me the freedom to create . . . and then sorting through the chaos of my creations to make a book. I don't know how you do it.

Big thanks to my agent, Jean Sagendorph, for steering this ship straight (instead of straight to crazytown).

I also have to mention all of the lovely women in my life who took care of my daughter in four-hour increments so I could write this book. Thank you for keeping my Camille happy by taking her on endless walks and letting her point out every flag, flower, and puppy. She is so lucky to be loved and lifted up by so many women. And I am so lucky to have all of you in my life.

Index